ZADAR, CI

Travel Guide 2025

Hidden Gems, Local Secrets, and Expert Tips for an
Unforgettable Adventure

James J. Lambert

Copyright Page

Disclaimer

The information in this book is for general informational and entertainment purposes only. While every effort has been made to ensure accuracy, the author and publisher make no warranties, express or implied, regarding the completeness, reliability, or suitability of the content. Readers are encouraged to verify details independently before making travel plans or decisions.

The author and publisher are not responsible for any loss, injury, or inconvenience resulting from the use of this book. Any reliance on the information provided is strictly at the reader's own risk. Views expressed are those of the author and do not constitute professional advice.

TABLE OF CONTENTS

General Map of Zadar, Croatia

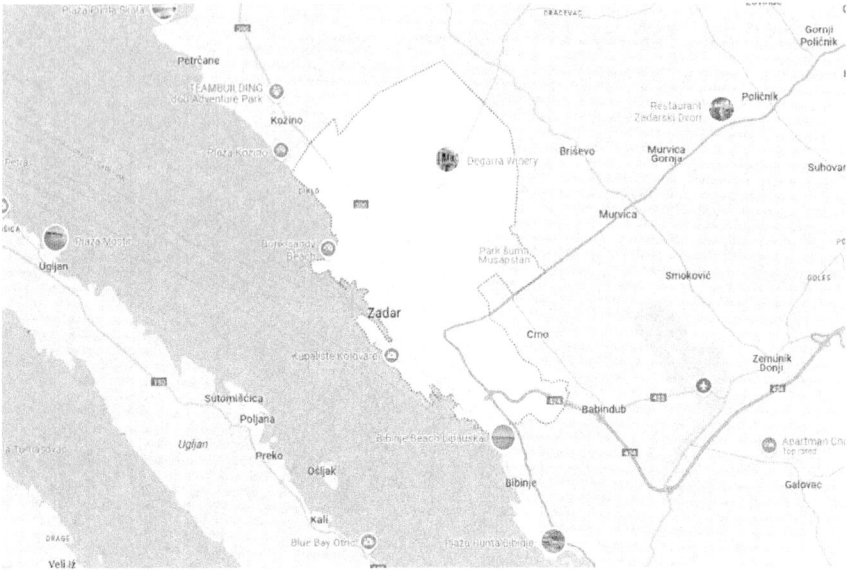

https://maps.app.goo.gl/1eJw3k498inrgxL48

Scan the QR-Code to see the real-time location.

Chapter 1: Introduction to Zadar

1.1 Welcome to Zadar

There's a sound in Zadar that you won't hear anywhere else in the world, notes born of the sea itself. As the Adriatic's waves lap against carefully engineered steps, the Sea Organ sighs a tune, and suddenly you're no longer just a visitor, you're a part of something ancient, something poetic.

Welcome to Zadar, a place where Roman ruins coexist with modern art installations, where medieval churches shadow open-air cafés, and where every sunset feels like a private performance. I first arrived in this coastal Croatian city on a whim, chasing whispers of terracotta roofs and turquoise seas. Years later, I still return, drawn back like the tide. This guide is a tribute to all that Zadar is, a living, breathing museum wrapped in Mediterranean ease.

Zadar isn't just a destination; it's a sensory journey. The salt on your lips after a morning swim. The scent of grilled calamari wafting through stone alleyways. The golden wash of late afternoon sun on the marble pavement. Whether you're a solo adventurer seeking silence, a couple chasing romance, or a family searching for something both playful and profound, Zadar unfolds to meet you.

1.2 Why Zadar? (Unique Attractions & Highlights)

Let's talk about why Zadar deserves a spot on your itinerary, perhaps even at the top. For starters, it has a soul. Unlike Dubrovnik's high-gloss allure or Split's boisterous crowds, Zadar moves at a gentler rhythm. It whispers rather than shouts.

Must-See Landmarks That Stay With You

- **Sea Organ (Morske Orgulje)** – An architectural wonder, this wave-powered instrument creates haunting, harmonic tones. Sit on the marble steps at sunset, and you'll understand why locals consider this their sanctuary.

- **Greeting to the Sun (Pozdrav Suncu)** – Just beside the Sea Organ, this solar-powered light installation pulses with color after dark, mimicking the rhythm of the universe above. It's both a spectacle and a meditation.

- **Church of St. Donatus** – A round, ninth-century church that's become Zadar's architectural icon. Step inside and listen to your footsteps echo through a thousand years of history.

- **Roman Forum** – History beneath your feet. Ancient stones form the skeleton of the city, where children now play and locals sip espresso.

Hidden Gems Worth Discovering

- **Kolovare Beach** – A short stroll from the city center, perfect for a morning dip. The Adriatic here is crystalline and calm.

- **Narodni Trg (People's Square)** – Buzzing with life but rarely packed, this is the heart of local life, best explored with a coffee in hand and no agenda.

Zadar rewards the curious. Stray from the main streets and you'll find tiny artisan shops selling handwoven lace or olive oils from nearby groves. Take a ferry to Ugljan island for a day of hiking and sea views, or explore the nearby Paklenica National Park for a taste of Croatia's rugged beauty.

1.3 A Brief History of Zadar

Zadar's timeline reads like a tale of survival and reinvention. Founded by the Liburnians, fortified by the Romans, shaped by Venetians, bombed during World War II, and reborn in modern Croatia, it's a city that has absorbed every era into its stonework.

Walk through the Old Town, and history hums beneath your shoes. You'll spot Roman columns reused in medieval buildings, and Venetian lions carved into city gates.

The Church of St. Mary, dating back to the 11th century, shares a street with Austro-Hungarian architecture. Each chapter of Zadar's past is layered on the last, not erased but embraced.

For history lovers, I recommend a visit to the Archaeological Museum, where Neolithic tools, Roman pottery, and medieval artifacts tell the city's story in quiet detail. Or explore St. Anastasia's Cathedral, the largest in Dalmatia, whose bell tower offers sweeping views of the entire peninsula.

1.4 Best Time to Visit (Seasonal Overview)

Zadar is blessed with over 2,500 hours of sunshine a year, but each season brings a different side of the city to life.

Spring (March to May)
Spring is perhaps my favorite time here. The air is fragrant with blooming rosemary and citrus blossoms, and the city begins to stir from its winter slumber. It's warm enough to enjoy outdoor cafés but cool enough for hiking and sightseeing.

Summer (June to August)
This is peak season, for good reason. Festivals light up the evenings, beaches are at their prime, and ferry routes are plentiful. Just know that popular spots get crowded. Book accommodations early, and don't be afraid to explore lesser-known islands or inland vineyards.

Autumn (September to October)

The weather remains warm, but the crowds thin. It's grape harvest season, and the Dalmatian coast glows with golden light. Ideal for couples or solo travelers seeking a more reflective trip.

Winter (November to February)

Zadar in winter is peaceful, almost sleepy. While some restaurants close, the cultural scene continues with concerts, Christmas markets, and art exhibitions. Accommodation prices drop, and locals have more time to chat, an underappreciated treasure of off-season travel.

1.5 Who This Guide Is For (Tailored Travel Tips for All Travelers)

I've written this guide for *you*, no matter your travel style. Zadar isn't a one-size-fits-all city, it's a mosaic of experiences, waiting to be shaped around your preferences.

For Families

Zadar is one of the most child-friendly cities I've traveled through. The Old Town is mostly pedestrian, the beaches are gentle, and there are endless gelato stops. Visit Veli Iž island for kayaking adventures or explore the Museum of Illusions for hands-on fun.

For Couples

Sunset here is not a cliché, it's a ritual. Find a seat near the Sea Organ, sip local wine, and let the magic unfold. Take a sunset cruise or wander hand-in-hand through the lantern-lit alleys after dinner at Pet Bunara or Proto Food & More.

For Solo Travelers

Zadar is safe, welcoming, and walkable. Join a local food tour or strike up a conversation in one of the wine bars tucked into the Old Town. I've made lifelong friends here over shared plates of black risotto.

For Budget Travelers

You don't need deep pockets to enjoy Zadar. Public beaches are free, street food like burek (savory pastry) is delicious and cheap, and the best experiences, like the Sea Organ or Roman Forum, don't cost a thing.

For Luxury Seekers

Indulge in a stay at Hotel Bastion, enjoy a private boat charter to the Kornati islands, or treat yourself to a seafood feast paired with award-winning Croatian wines. Zadar offers refinement in an understated, authentic way.

Your Zadar Story Begins Here

Whether you're arriving by plane, car, or sailing in with the wind at your back, Zadar greets you with an open heart and centuries of stories. This chapter is just the beginning, a compass pointing toward your own adventure.

In the pages that follow, I'll guide you deeper into Zadar's soul: its neighborhoods, flavors, landscapes, and rhythms. Prepare to be captivated, delighted, and perhaps even changed by what you discover here. Because once you hear the sea sing in Zadar, you'll never forget it.

Chapter 2: Essential Trip Planning

Planning your journey to Zadar is like laying the foundation for a story that's destined to become unforgettable. The city, with its ancient walls and Adriatic charm, rewards the prepared traveler with seamless days and memorable moments. I've wandered its sunlit alleys in July and watched the rain fall on its marble streets in December. With each visit, I learned a little more about how to navigate it smoothly, and now, I'm here to pass those insights along.

This chapter is your compass. Whether you're dreaming of summer sunsets or winter solitude, you'll find everything you need here to plan wisely and travel well.

2.1 Entry Requirements (Visas, Passports, Vaccinations)

Getting into Croatia is refreshingly straightforward, especially for travelers from Europe, North America, and many parts of Asia. However, it's always best to double-check your country's specific requirements before setting out.

Passports and Visas

- EU/EEA Citizens can enter Croatia with just a valid national ID card. No visa is needed.

- U.S., Canadian, Australian, and New Zealand Citizens can stay in Croatia for up to 90 days within 180 days without a visa.

- UK Citizens also enjoy visa-free travel for 90 days within any 180 days.

- Other Nationalities may require a Schengen visa, as Croatia joined the Schengen Area in January 2023. Check the latest requirements on Croatia's Ministry of Foreign and European Affairs website.

Make sure your passport is valid for at least three months beyond your planned departure date from the Schengen Zone.

Vaccinations & Health

No specific vaccinations are required for entry. Standard travel vaccinations, like Hepatitis A and B, and routine immunizations, are always advisable. Tap water is safe to drink in Zadar, and pharmacies are well-stocked for common needs.

2.2 When to Go: Seasons & Festivals

Each time of year in Zadar feels like stepping into a different novel. I've basked in summer's Mediterranean vibrance, wandered quiet lanes in winter mist, and joined locals for springtime festivals when the air is rich with citrus blossoms.

Spring (March–May)

The city begins to stretch and awaken. Fewer crowds, mild temperatures (13°C–21°C), and fields of wildflowers in nearby parks. Great for photography, hiking, and culture without the heat or bustle.

Summer (June–August)

Peak season, and it shows. Zadar pulses with life. Expect sunny days averaging 27°C, crowded beaches, lively cafés, and festivals under the stars. Plan ahead for accommodations and reservations.

Autumn (September–October)

Still warm (20°C–25°C) and far less crowded. The Adriatic is warm enough to swim in, and harvest season brings wine tastings, olive oil festivals, and a golden glow over the stone streets.

Winter (November–February)

Quiet, contemplative Zadar. Fewer tourists, lower prices, and a city that feels entirely yours. I love Zadar in December, festive markets, mulled wine, and candlelit dinners tucked in ancient buildings. Note: Some island ferries and tours run on limited schedules in winter.

Don't Miss These Festivals:

- **Zadar Summer Theatre Festival (July–August)** – Live performances across the city, from dance to classical music.

- **Night of the Full Moon (August)** – The Riva turns into a night market of lanterns, folklore, and fresh seafood under moonlight.

- **Musical Evenings in St. Donatus (July)** – Classical concerts inside one of the oldest pre-Romanesque churches in Europe.

2.3 How Long to Stay in Zadar

I'm often asked, "How many days do I need in Zadar?" The answer depends on how deeply you want to dive in.

The Quick Explorer: 2–3 Days
Enough time to see the Sea Organ, stroll the Roman Forum, enjoy a swim at Kolovare Beach, and taste local seafood.

The Immersive Traveler: 4–5 Days
Add island hopping to Ugljan or Dugi Otok, day trips to Plitvice Lakes or Krka National Park, and long dinners over Dalmatian wine.

The Culture Seeker: 1 Week+
Combine Zadar with nearby destinations like Šibenik, Nin, or Pag Island. Soak in both the coastal calm and inland charm.

Tip: I recommend staying within or just outside the Old Town. The walkability and ambiance are worth every kuna (or now, every euro).

2.4 What to Pack: Seasonal Essentials

Packing for Zadar isn't complicated, but a few thoughtful items can make all the difference.

Spring & Autumn Essentials

- Light layers (mornings and evenings can be cool)
- Comfortable walking shoes (Zadar's stone streets can be slippery)
- A waterproof jacket for unexpected rain
- Sunglasses and a hat (yes, even in spring)

Summer Must-Haves

- Breathable clothing
- Swimsuits (plural, you'll want a dry one for sunset dips)
- Reef-friendly sunscreen
- A power adapter (Croatia uses 230V, type C and F plugs)
- A reusable water bottle, hydration is key, and fountains are everywhere

Winter Suggestions

- A warm coat and scarf (temps can dip to 5°C)

- Layers, including sweaters and waterproof shoes

- A small umbrella and gloves

Don't Forget:

- Travel insurance (for peace of mind)

- Offline maps or translation apps (Wi-Fi is widely available, but it's nice to be prepared)

- A daypack for island excursions or city strolls

2.5 Accessibility & Traveler Support Services

Zadar is making great strides in accessibility, but like many historic European cities, some areas still pose challenges for travelers with mobility concerns. That said, with a little preparation, the city is navigable and welcoming to all.

For Travelers with Limited Mobility

- **Old Town Streets:** While cobblestones dominate, many main thoroughfares are flat and wide. The Riva promenade is particularly accessible.

- **Public Transportation:** Most buses are modern and equipped with ramps. Drivers are helpful, though not always fluent in English.

- **Accommodations:** Many hotels and apartments offer accessible rooms, just confirm details ahead of time.

- **Accessible Attractions:** The Sea Organ, Greeting to the Sun, museums, and churches like St. Donatus are partially or fully accessible.

Medical Services & Support

- Zadar has a public hospital and several private clinics. English is commonly spoken among medical staff.

- Pharmacies are plentiful and well-stocked, marked with a green cross. One is always open 24 hours on rotation (details usually posted in the window).

LGBTQ+ Travelers

Zadar is relatively conservative but friendly. Public displays of affection may draw stares in rural areas but are generally accepted in tourist zones. Croatia legally protects LGBTQ+ rights, and the travel scene is welcoming, particularly among younger locals and expats.

Solo Travelers

Zadar is one of the safest places I've traveled solo. Locals are helpful, crime is low, and the atmosphere is calm. Still, follow the usual precautions, secure valuables, and trust your instincts.

A Trip That Starts Strong, Ends Sweeter

Zadar is easy to fall into, and even easier to navigate when you're armed with a bit of insider know-how. From the moment your passport is stamped to your final sip of rakija at a harbor-side bar, this city invites you to travel smart, slow, and deeply.

Chapter 3: Getting There and Around

There's something about the moment you arrive in Zadar that feels almost cinematic, like a slow pan across a marble-clad stage set beneath the Adriatic sky. Whether you glide in by ferry under the golden light of sunset, descend through a patchwork of Croatian coastline by air, or drive through pine-scented hills, your first glimpse of Zadar will likely be unforgettable. As someone who has approached this city by land, air, and sea, I can tell you: every arrival has its magic.

But the beauty of Zadar isn't just in its destination, it's in the ease with which you can move through it. Compact yet full of character, Zadar invites exploration on foot, by bicycle, or via its efficient transport system. In this chapter, we'll navigate the ins and outs of getting here and getting around, so your journey begins with clarity and confidence.

3.1 How to Reach Zadar (Air, Land, Sea)

By Air: Zadar Airport (ZAD)

Zadar Airport, just 12 kilometers from the city center, is a small but mighty hub that connects travelers to dozens of European cities, particularly during the high season.

I've flown into ZAD many times, and what always strikes me is its efficiency, within 30 minutes of landing, I'm usually sipping coffee along the Riva promenade.

- **Airlines:** Ryanair, Lufthansa, Croatia Airlines, and Eurowings dominate here, offering budget-friendly routes from London, Berlin, Vienna, and more.

- **Transportation from Airport to City:**

  - **Airport Shuttle:** Operated by Liburnija Zadar, the shuttle runs every 30 minutes during peak times and drops passengers at the main bus station and city center.

  - **Taxi:** About 25-30 EUR, with a travel time of 15–20 minutes.

  - **Rental Cars:** Available onsite from major providers like Sixt, Hertz, and Avantcar.

By Land: Bus and Car

If you're already exploring Croatia or the Balkans, reaching Zadar by bus or car is a breeze.

- **Buses:** Zadar's main bus terminal is well connected to cities like Zagreb (3.5 hrs), Split (2.5 hrs), Rijeka (4 hrs), and even international destinations like Ljubljana or Sarajevo. Buses are modern, comfortable, and punctual.

- **Driving:** The A1 highway makes driving into Zadar smooth and scenic. Parking in the Old Town can be limited, but newer lots on its outskirts offer ample space and affordable rates.

By Sea: Ferry & Catamaran

Zadar's coastal charm is amplified when you approach it by sea.

- **Domestic Ferries:** Jadrolinija offers connections to nearby islands such as Ugljan, Dugi Otok, and Premuda, perfect for day trips or relaxed getaways.

- **International Lines:** Seasonal routes connect Zadar with Ancona in Italy, typically between June and September.

3.2 Transportation Within the City (Buses, Taxis, Walking, Bike Rentals)

Zadar isn't the kind of city that demands grand infrastructure to get around, it invites you to slow down, wander, and let its ancient stones guide you.

On Foot: Best for the Old Town

The historic heart of Zadar is a pedestrian's paradise. Narrow alleyways, open squares, Roman ruins, and café-lined streets make walking the most intimate and satisfying way to explore.

- Must-see spots like St. Donatus Church, the Sea Organ, and Five Wells Square are all within a short walking radius.

- Wear sturdy shoes, Zadar's marble paving stones are beautiful but slippery when wet.

Buses: Liburnija Zadar

The local bus network is efficient, clean, and reasonably priced. Tickets can be purchased from kiosks or directly from drivers.

- **Bus No. 2** connects the city center with Borik (great for beaches).

- **Bus No. 9** links the Old Town with the main bus terminal.

- A single ride costs around 1.60 EUR if bought at a kiosk, slightly more onboard.

Taxis & Ride-Sharing

Taxis are widely available but can be pricey for short distances. Ensure the meter is running or agree on a price before the ride.

- Bolt and Uber are operational in Zadar and are often cheaper and more convenient than traditional taxis.

Bicycle Rentals

Zadar's flat terrain and coastal roads make cycling both scenic and practical.

- Nextbike offers public bike-sharing stations throughout the city.

- Local shops also rent bikes by the hour or day, with maps for self-guided routes.

- Ride along the Kolovare promenade at sunrise, it's a memory in the making.

3.3 Navigational Tools (Maps, Apps, Tourist Cards)

When I first visited Zadar, I relied on a paper map folded into my back pocket. Today, technology offers simpler and smarter options.

Navigation Apps

- **Google Maps**: Highly reliable, especially for walking directions in the Old Town.

- **Moovit**: Excellent for local bus routes and schedules.

- **Offline Maps**: Apps like Maps.me or the downloaded areas feature in Google Maps are lifesavers if your data coverage is patchy.

Tourist Cards

The Zadar Card (seasonally available) is a great option for travelers wanting to dig deeper while saving money.

- Includes free or discounted entry to museums (like the Archaeological Museum of Zadar), public transport, and guided tours.

- Available in 1-day, 3-day, or 7-day passes.

- Check with the Zadar Tourist Board or local info centers for current pricing and benefits.

Printed Guides & Maps

Don't underestimate the value of a well-designed paper map, especially when exploring historical landmarks. Many hotels and tourist offices offer beautifully illustrated versions highlighting walking routes, museums, and dining recommendations.

3.4 Sustainable Transportation Options

Zadar is quietly making moves toward a more sustainable tourism model, and visitors can easily take part in that journey.

Public Transport Over Private Cars

Buses and bikes reduce congestion and emissions, and they also allow you to see more of the city through a local lens.

Walking Tours with a Twist

Several local outfits offer eco-conscious walking tours, including food tours focused on seasonal Dalmatian cuisine and historical walks led by local university students.

Electric Scooters & Green Bikes

In recent years, electric scooters have become a common sight. They're affordable, fun, and can be rented via smartphone apps like Bolt or Lime.

Responsible Boating

Planning an island trip? Choose boat operators that promote sustainable practices. Look for smaller group sizes, eco-certified companies, and itineraries that respect marine conservation zones.

Let the Journey Flow

Reaching Zadar is only the beginning, but getting around once you're here is part of what makes this place so delightfully livable. The city invites you to walk slowly, linger at corners, and discover hidden gems tucked between ancient stone walls. Whether you hop a bus to a nearby beach, cycle along the coast, or wander through centuries-old alleys, you'll find the rhythm of Zadar isn't in rushing, it's in roaming.

Chapter 4: Where to Stay

For me, where I stay is never just a place to sleep. It's the soul of the trip, the quiet courtyard where I sip morning coffee, the scent of sea salt drifting through an open window, the rhythm of footsteps in a cobbled alley outside my door. In Zadar, your accommodation isn't merely a pit stop between sightseeing sprees; it becomes part of the narrative.

In this chapter, I'll walk you through Zadar's neighborhoods and help you find the perfect place to stay, whether you're a solo backpacker, a couple seeking romance, a family with little ones in tow, or a luxury traveler looking to soak up Adriatic splendor in style.

4.1 Overview of Zadar's Neighborhoods

Zadar is a city of contrast, old and new, coastal and urban, serene and bustling. Understanding its layout helps tailor your stay to your travel style.

- **Old Town (Poluotok):** This is Zadar's beating heart, a peninsula wrapped in Roman ruins, Venetian palaces, and lively piazzas. Staying here puts you steps from iconic sites like the Sea Organ and the Greeting to the Sun.

It's ideal for first-time visitors, culture lovers, and those who enjoy walking.

- **Borik:** About 3 km northwest of the Old Town, Borik is known for its beaches, family-friendly resorts, and sunset views. It's quieter and offers more space, perfect for those prioritizing relaxation and seaside leisure.

- **Diklo:** Further west from Borik, this residential neighborhood is more local and peaceful, offering private apartments and a slower pace of life.

- **Relja & Kolovare:** Just outside the Old Town walls, these areas are convenient and well-connected. They offer a mix of modern hotels and budget-friendly apartments.

4.2 Budget-Friendly Lodging (Hostels, Guesthouses)

If you're traveling on a shoestring or simply prefer spending your kunas on wine and excursions rather than four-poster beds, Zadar has excellent budget options.

- **The Lazy Monkey Hostel:** Located near the beach in Borik, this is a lively, social space perfect for solo travelers. Think hammocks, beanbags, nightly BBQs, and a laid-back backpacker vibe.

- **Downtown Boutique Hostel:** Right in the heart of the Old Town, this stylish, clean, and surprisingly affordable spot offers both dorms and private rooms.

- **Guesthouse Barba:** Tucked away in a quiet street near Kolovare Beach, Barba is a family-run pension with warm hospitality and spotless rooms.

Tip: Book a budget stay early during summer. Zadar is increasingly popular among backpackers, and beds fill up quickly from June through August.

4.3 Mid-Range Hotels & Boutique Stays

For those who appreciate comfort without extravagance, Zadar's mid-range scene is brimming with charming boutique hotels and stylish apartments.

- **Art Hotel Kalelarga:** Located right on Zadar's famous main street, Široka ulica, this hotel doubles as a gallery. Each room is a tribute to Zadar's history, adorned with locally inspired art.

- **Teatro Verdi Boutique Hotel:** With its sophisticated aesthetic and exceptional service, this spot near the Roman Forum is a hidden gem for couples.

- **Villa Diana Zadar:** Nestled in Borik, Villa Diana offers cozy studios and a lush garden, a tranquil refuge after a day of sightseeing.

Expect air conditioning, reliable Wi-Fi, and an on-site breakfast in most mid-range options, and some even include complimentary bike rentals or access to small spas.

4.4 Luxury Accommodations (Resorts, Seaside Hotels)

If you're here to indulge, perhaps celebrating a honeymoon, anniversary, or just your well-earned vacation, Zadar doesn't disappoint.

- **Falkensteiner Hotel & Spa Iadera:** Just north of the city in Punta Skala, this five-star retreat is a haven of wellness. Expect infinity pools, Adriatic views, gourmet dining, and a world-class spa.

- **Bastion Heritage Hotel:** Set in an 18th-century fortress in the Old Town, Bastion is both historic and luxurious. Their fine-dining restaurant and stone-clad spa are standouts.

- **Hotel Kolovare:** Overlooking Zadar's main beach, this modern hotel offers comfort with a sea breeze. Ideal for families and business travelers alike.

Local Insight: Luxury in Zadar often means understated elegance, with an emphasis on natural materials, sustainability, and seamless service.

4.5 Unique & Alternative Stays (Eco-Lodges, Airbnb, Heritage Buildings)

Sometimes, you want something with character, a place that tells a story.

- **Airbnbs in the Old Town:** From loft apartments above ancient Roman roads to modern flats with exposed stone walls and original frescoes, Zadar's Airbnbs offer unique stays full of charm.

- **Eco-Village Zrmanja:** Just outside Zadar, this off-the-grid retreat offers wooden cabins, a permaculture garden, and outdoor adventure opportunities like kayaking and hiking. Perfect for nature lovers.

- **Stays in Heritage Buildings:** Some local guesthouses operate inside protected heritage homes, where you might sleep beneath wooden beams from the 15th century or open shutters that frame views of medieval spires.

Travel Tip: When booking Airbnbs or heritage stays, read reviews carefully for notes on air conditioning, noise levels, and stair access. Historic charm often comes with quirks.

Choose a Place That Reflects Your Journey

There's a place for every traveler in Zadar, and each accommodation style offers its own flavor of the city. If you're visiting for the first time and want to be in the middle of the action, the Old Town will never disappoint. If it's the lapping of waves and morning swims you seek, head toward Borik or Diklo. And if your soul craves something truly distinct, stay in a stone house where centuries echo through every creak of the floorboards.

Where you rest your head can set the tone for your entire experience. Choose a stay that doesn't just suit your budget, but one that reflects your way of traveling, your pace, and your purpose.

Chapter 5: Top Attractions & Unmissable Landmarks

If I had to pick just one reason travelers fall head over heels for Zadar, it would be this: the city is an open-air museum with a modern soul. Here, you can sip coffee on Roman ruins, witness the sun set to the rhythm of a sea-powered symphony, or walk along sun-bleached stones that have guided footsteps for over 3,000 years. In this chapter, we'll stroll through Zadar's most captivating landmarks, those that stir your imagination, catch your breath, and stay with you long after you've left.

5.1 Sea Organ & Sun Salutation

Two Modern Icons with an Ancient Backdrop

Let's start at the edge of the Old Town, where the Adriatic meets art and architecture in two spellbinding experiences: the Sea Organ (Morske orgulje) and the Sun Salutation (Pozdrav Suncu).

The Sea Organ, designed by architect Nikola Bašić, is a 70-meter-long architectural installation built into the marble steps descending into the sea. Beneath those steps lies a system of pipes and resonant chambers that "play" music as waves wash through them.

The sound is otherworldly, ethereal, melancholic, and entirely unpredictable. I've spent many evenings here, letting the soundscape wash over me as sailboats bob on the horizon and the sky erupts into gold and lavender.

Just a few steps away, you'll find the Sun Salutation, another of Bašić's masterpieces. This circular solar panel embedded into the stone plaza absorbs sunlight by day and transforms it into a dazzling light show after dusk. As darkness falls, the plaza comes alive with hypnotic patterns that echo the rhythms of the sea and stars. Children dance on it. Couples linger. Photographers gather like moths to a flame.

Travel Tips:

- Visit at sunset for the full sensory experience: visual, auditory, and emotional.

- Go early in the morning if you want quiet contemplation with just the sounds of the waves.

5.2 Roman Forum & St. Donatus Church

Where the Past Speaks Through Stone

From the water's edge, wander into the heart of Zadar's Old Town, and you'll find yourself walking in the footsteps of Roman governors, medieval bishops, and modern-day flâneurs.

The Roman Forum is the largest in Croatia and dates back to the 1st century BCE. Today, it's an open plaza strewn with marble columns, half-buried pedestals, and the skeletal remains of temples. What I love most is how seamlessly it blends into modern life, you'll see kids playing hide-and-seek among the ruins while tourists sketch and locals chat over coffee.

Towering beside the forum is the Church of St. Donatus, a round, pre-Romanesque marvel from the 9th century. Its raw stone walls and austere beauty are a reminder of early Christianity's deep roots in Dalmatia. Though it no longer serves religious functions, it occasionally hosts classical music concerts thanks to its outstanding acoustics.

Don't Miss:

- Climb the bell tower of St. Anastasia's Cathedral next door for stunning rooftop views.

- Visit at twilight when the golden light dances across ancient stone.

5.3 Museums and Cultural Spaces

Where Zadar's Soul Is Preserved

For such a compact city, Zadar has a remarkably rich museum scene. Each one offers a window into the region's layered history, from its Roman foundations to its modern-day reinvention.

Archaeological Museum: Situated just off the Roman Forum, this is one of Croatia's most important archaeological collections. Highlights include Roman glassware, Illyrian jewelry, and detailed models of ancient Zadar.

Museum of Ancient Glass: A personal favorite. Housed in a restored 19th-century palace, it showcases stunning glass artifacts and even features live glassblowing demonstrations. It's both educational and mesmerizing.

National Museum of Zadar: This multi-department museum includes the Ethnological Section, which explores traditional Dalmatian life through costumes, crafts, and recreated homes.

Art Galleries and Contemporary Spaces:

- Check out the City Gallery for modern and contemporary art exhibits.

- The Museum of Illusions offers a quirky break for families or those craving something interactive.

Local Insight:

Many museums offer combined tickets or discounts with a Zadar City Card, which also includes bus fare and discounts at restaurants.

5.4 Beaches & Natural Landscapes

Where Nature Weaves into the Urban Fabric

Zadar isn't all stone and history, it's blessed with a coastline too. And while the beaches here may be pebbled rather than sandy, they're stunningly clear and refreshingly uncrowded compared to more famous Dalmatian destinations.

Kolovare Beach:

The closest beach to the Old Town, Kolovare, is a mix of pebbles, pine trees, and concrete sunbathing decks. It's well-equipped, family-friendly, and offers shaded areas, perfect for a midday dip after exploring.

Borik Beach:

Located in a more residential zone, Borik is known for its shallow water, beach bars, and water sports. If you're traveling with children or seeking a laid-back day in the sun, this is your spot.

Puntamika Peninsula:

A quieter area with fantastic views back toward the Old Town skyline. Ideal for a peaceful swim or a romantic sunset picnic.

Nearby Natural Escapes:

- Telašćica Nature Park (on Dugi Otok island): Cliffs, salt lakes, and unspoiled coves.

- Paklenica National Park (a 1-hour drive): A paradise for hikers and rock climbers, with dramatic canyons and pine-covered trails.

Pro Tip:

Water shoes help navigate rocky beaches, and early morning swims offer calm waters and local company.

5.5 Best Panoramic Views & Photography Spots

The City in Frames and Vistas

Zadar's beauty reveals itself in angles, arched alleyways, golden-hour bell towers, and Adriatic blues that seem surreal.

Bell Tower of St. Anastasia's Cathedral:

Climbing this medieval tower rewards you with a bird's-eye view of the red-roofed city unfolding toward the sea. Time your climb for late afternoon when shadows lengthen and the light is soft.

Riva Promenade at Sunset:

Zadar's sunsets are legendary, Alfred Hitchcock once called them the most beautiful in the world. Walk along the Riva with a gelato in hand or simply sit on the sea wall and watch the sky burn.

Foša Harbor:

A charming, lesser-known spot just outside the city gates. The old stone bridge, turquoise water, and boats moored under palm trees create a postcard-worthy scene.

Zadar Bridge (Gradski Most):

Cross this pedestrian bridge for a panoramic shot of the Old Town skyline, especially stunning in the golden morning light or twinkling evening glow.

A City Etched in Memory

Zadar's greatest gift is how effortlessly it blends centuries of history with the pulse of modern life. You'll wander ancient streets guided by the music of the sea, pause before Roman stones that whisper stories, and find beauty not just in the landmarks but in the spaces between.

Whether you're capturing that perfect photo, soaking in sea sounds, or gazing up at a star-streaked sky, these are the moments that turn a trip into a memory.

Chapter 6: Hidden Gems & Local Favorites

There's something undeniably thrilling about peeling back the layers of a city and discovering the quiet magic that doesn't always make it onto glossy brochures. Zadar may dazzle you with its iconic Sea Organ and ancient forum, but it's in the lesser-known corners and unscripted moments that you'll truly fall under its spell. In this chapter, I'll take you on a journey beyond the postcard-perfect facades, into the secret courtyards, tucked-away beaches, artisan workshops, and wild beauty of the Zadar hinterland, the parts of this Adriatic gem that locals cherish and visitors never forget.

6.1 Secret Courtyards & Alleys

The Charm Behind the Stone

Wandering Zadar's Old Town is like meandering through a maze built from history itself. But step off the main streets, and you'll start to uncover quiet courtyards draped in vines, sleepy alleys that seem to pause time, and secret corners where life plays out unhurried.

One of my favorite discoveries is the small courtyard behind the Rector's Palace.

While most people stop at the museum's entrance or café terrace, walk around to the rear and you'll find a peaceful space where fig trees cast dappled shade and the soft trickle of a hidden fountain muffles the city's bustle.

Near Five Wells Square, there's a narrow stone alley, often overlooked, called Perivoj kraljice Jelene Madijevke that opens onto a park built atop the old Venetian bastion. The view from here stretches over terracotta roofs and out to the sea, but the best part is the silence. It's one of my go-to spots to journal, sketch, or simply breathe.

Tips for Exploration:

- Go early in the morning or during siesta hours (2–5 PM) when the Old Town slows down.

- Bring a small camera or sketchbook to capture details, cracked tiles, ivy-covered walls, and laundry swaying between balconies.

6.2 Hidden Beaches & Nature Escapes

Beyond the Crowds, Where the Adriatic Whispers

Zadar's coastline is no secret, but veer off the usual routes and you'll find intimate spots where the sea sparkles just for you.

One such place is Plaža Puntamika, a small pebble cove tucked away behind the lighthouse on the peninsula. You'll need to weave past a few residential streets to get there, but the reward is a tranquil beach framed by pine trees and with a pristine view of the Old Town across the water.

For something even more secluded, hop on a ferry to Ugljan Island and head to Kukljica. From there, hike 15 minutes through the woods to Sabuša Beach, a shallow, emerald-colored bay that's perfect for swimming and picnicking. It's beloved by locals, especially at sunset, when the sea glows and fishermen return to the harbor with the day's catch.

Another gem is Veliko Blato Nature Reserve, just a 30-minute drive from Zadar. A birdwatcher's paradise, this freshwater lake and wetland area sees flamingos, herons, and rare migratory birds. It's peaceful, wild, and completely off the radar for most tourists.

Nature Essentials:

- Water shoes for rocky beaches.

- A reusable water bottle and reef-safe sunscreen.

- Light snacks and a towel for impromptu swims.

6.3 Authentic Local Experiences (Workshops, Artisan Shops)

Craftsmanship and Creativity You Can Take Home

While souvenirs of seashell magnets and mass-produced trinkets are easy to find, Zadar is also home to a thriving artisan scene, if you know where to look.

Tucked into a quiet lane just off Kalelarga is Zlatarevo Zlato, a family-run jewelry workshop that has been crafting filigree and traditional Dalmatian designs for generations. The artisans are usually happy to explain the meaning behind each motif, and if you're lucky, they might even give you a peek behind the curtain of their craft.

Then there's Art Hotel Kalelarga, not just a place to stay but also a cultural space where you can sometimes join ceramic or printmaking workshops held in their small studio. These sessions are intimate and hands-on, and you get to take your own artwork home, a perfect, personal memento of your time in Zadar.

For food lovers, I highly recommend joining a cooking class with a local chef. A few small outfits offer classes in traditional Dalmatian cuisine, think pašticada (beef stew in red wine and prunes), soparnik (chard-filled flatbread), and homemade rakija (fruit brandy).

Cooking alongside locals in a stone courtyard kitchen is the kind of memory that lingers long after your trip.

Where to Look:

- Zadar Tourist Info offers up-to-date listings on workshops.

- Local hotels and boutique stays often have partnerships with artisans or chefs.

6.4 Exploring the Zadar Hinterland

Where Vineyards, Villages, and Ruins Await

Just inland from Zadar lies a different world, quieter, greener, and steeped in rural tradition. The hinterland is one of my favorite escapes when I need to slow down and connect with Croatia's agricultural and cultural roots.

Start in Ravni Kotari, a fertile plain where vineyards and olive groves roll out in every direction. Here, you can visit family-owned wineries like Degarra or MasVin, both of which offer tastings and tours. The wines are excellent, crisp whites, bold reds, and are usually paired with locally made cheese, prosciutto, and olive oil.

Nearby, the village of Nadin offers a glimpse into traditional life. It's not unusual to see locals harvesting grapes by hand, or to stumble upon a weekend festival where folk dancing and roast lamb are the stars of the show.

One of the most underappreciated sites in the region is the Asseria Ruins, near the town of Benkovac. This ancient Roman city, once a major stronghold, is slowly being unearthed, and walking through its silent stone gates feels like stepping into a forgotten chapter of history.

How to Explore:

- Rent a car for a day trip or book a guided rural tour with a focus on food and culture.

- Wear good walking shoes and bring cash, many village businesses don't take cards.

Finding the Heart of Zadar

Zadar's true spirit isn't confined to its main attractions or sunny postcards, it lives in the hush of its hidden courtyards, the hush of secret beaches, and the warm chatter in a local kitchen. Whether you're marveling at a handmade necklace, sharing wine under the olive trees, or watching herons glide over a remote lake, these are the experiences that transform a trip into a journey.

Chapter 7: Savoring Zadar – Food & Drink

There's a rhythm to Zadar that's best understood through its flavors. Each bite carries a whisper of the Adriatic, a scent of olive groves bathed in sunlight, a memory of Sunday lunches prepared with generations-old love. From rustic taverns tucked into ancient alleyways to chic seaside cafés where cocktails meet the sunset, Zadar is a city to be tasted as much as it is seen. In this chapter, I'll guide you through the culinary soul of Zadar, where to eat, what to drink, and how to savor every mouthful like a local.

7.1 Must-Try Dalmatian Dishes

Where Tradition Meets the Table

When you sit down to eat in Zadar, you're not just consuming a meal, you're stepping into a narrative woven from sea, soil, and centuries of culinary tradition. Dalmatian cuisine is rooted in simplicity and quality. Think fresh seafood, slow-cooked meats, seasonal vegetables, wild herbs, and olive oil that tastes like liquid gold.

Start your culinary exploration with brudet, a rich fish stew simmered in tomato, wine, and garlic, served with creamy polenta. It's a dish best enjoyed at a konoba (traditional tavern), preferably one overlooking the water. Another essential is pašticada, beef marinated in vinegar and wine for days, then slow-cooked with prunes and cloves. Served with gnocchi, it's the epitome of Dalmatian comfort food.

Don't miss:

- **Black risotto (crni rižot):** Squid ink lends this dish its dramatic color and briny depth. Best enjoyed with a glass of local white wine.

- **Peka:** Meat or octopus cooked under a bell-shaped lid buried in hot embers. You'll need to order this in advance at some restaurants.

- **Pag cheese (Paški sir):** A hard sheep's milk cheese with a salty tang from the island of Pag, just north of Zadar.

- **Fritule:** Small fried dough balls dusted with powdered sugar, often flavored with lemon zest or rakija (fruit brandy).

The beauty of eating in Zadar is that these traditional dishes don't feel dated, they're lovingly preserved and celebrated, whether at a family kitchen or a modern bistro.

7.2 Best Restaurants for Every Budget

Dining Delights for Every Traveler

One of the joys of Zadar is that you don't need to spend a fortune to eat well. Whether you're a backpacker on a shoestring or a traveler seeking a five-star meal, there's something here for every appetite and wallet.

Budget Bites:

- **Konoba Stomorica:** A no-frills local favorite serving hearty portions of grilled sardines, squid, and Dalmatian prosciutto at excellent prices.

- **Pizzeria Tri Bunara:** Located near the Three Wells, this pizzeria is a magnet for locals and offers wood-fired pizzas and pasta dishes under €10.

Mid-Range Favorites:

- **Pet Bunara:** A standout for sustainable, seasonal cuisine with a modern twist. Their slow-roasted lamb and homemade pasta are unforgettable.

- **Bruschetta Restaurant:** Just steps from the sea, this spot serves creative Mediterranean plates in a relaxed setting, ideal for sunset dinners.

High-End Indulgence:

- **Foša:** An upscale seafood restaurant perched by the city walls with a stunning view of the harbor. Fresh catch is artfully prepared with a refined Dalmatian flair. Perfect for a romantic splurge.

- **Kaštel Restaurant:** Set in a 13th-century fortress and offering gourmet tasting menus that showcase local ingredients in elegant style.

Regardless of your budget, always ask about the "daily catch" or "plate of the day" (dnevni meni), these often offers the best taste and value.

7.3 Wine Bars, Cafés & Cocktails by the Sea

Raise a Glass to the Zadar Sunset

If food is the heartbeat of Zadar, then its cafés and bars are where the city breathes, slowly, rhythmically, and always with a view. Whether it's your first coffee of the day or your third glass of wine, Zadar's drink culture is as much about the setting as it is about the sips.

Wine & Tapas:

- **Degarra Wine Bar:** Sleek and intimate, this is one of the best places to sample local wines like Pošip, Plavac Mali, and Maraština, all grown in Dalmatian soil.

- **The Garden Lounge:** A relaxed, boho-chic space with plush cushions, DJ sets, and a wide range of organic wines and craft beers.

Cafés with Character:

- **Caffe Bar Sv. Lovre:** Tucked behind St. Lawrence Church, this shaded courtyard café is perfect for a morning espresso or an afternoon prosecco.

- **Coffee & Cake:** A newer favorite among locals, offering artisan brews, homemade desserts, and Instagram-worthy lattes.

Cocktail Hour:

- **Ledana Lounge & Bar:** Nestled in Queen Jelena Madije Park, this stylish open-air lounge is known for its creative cocktails and lush surroundings.

- **Hedonist Dining & Hangout:** A trendy, modern bar where bartenders whip up craft drinks with local herbs and ingredients, think lavender gin or rosemary mojitos.

7.4 Food Markets & Gourmet Tours

From Market Stalls to Culinary Stories

To truly understand Zadar's food culture, head to its vibrant markets where locals shop daily for seafood, vegetables, cheeses, and olive oils. The Zadar Green Market (Tržnica) near the Old Town is a feast for the senses, alive with the scent of basil and the colors of ripe tomatoes and figs.

Visit in the early morning when fishermen bring in their catch, and you'll see locals haggling over the freshest squid, anchovies, and mussels. Stop by one of the small kiosks for a burek (savory pastry) or pick up local honey, dried lavender, or candied orange peel as edible souvenirs.

If you're curious to go deeper, culinary walking tours are a fantastic way to blend sightseeing with tastings. I recommend tours that include:

- Market visits with local guides.

- Olive oil and wine tastings.

- Traditional dessert samplings like rožata (a local flan).

- A stop at a konoba with a behind-the-scenes peek into Dalmatian kitchen traditions.

Tours are especially valuable for learning about local etiquette, like why it's polite to clink glasses and look your companions in the eye when toasting, or why rakija is more than just a drink, it's a ritual.

Tasting the True Zadar

Eating in Zadar is more than a necessity, it's a deeply immersive cultural experience. Whether you're nibbling cheese in a stone cellar, sipping wine as the sun melts into the sea, or cracking into fresh crab on a fishing dock, every moment is rich with authenticity and story. This city doesn't just feed you, it welcomes you to the table as a guest, and before long, as a friend.

Chapter 8: Shopping & Souvenirs

Zadar is a city where history and craftsmanship converge, where you can take home a piece of its soul in the form of carefully curated souvenirs. As you wander through the cobbled streets, you'll find yourself drawn into a world of local markets, artisan boutiques, and charming shops filled with treasures from the heart of Dalmatia. In this chapter, I'll share some of the best places to shop in Zadar and what to look for when you want to bring home a little bit of this ancient coastal city.

8.1 Local Markets & Artisan Boutiques

A Feast for the Senses

If you're anything like me, markets are the best place to start any shopping adventure. They offer not just items for sale, but also a window into the local culture. In Zadar, the Green Market (Tržnica) is a must-visit. Located just outside the Old Town, this bustling market is where the locals come to shop for fresh produce, seafood, and flowers. It's a kaleidoscope of colors: bright red tomatoes, deep purple eggplants, and golden honeycomb stacked high in the sunshine.

Here, you can pick up a bottle of local olive oil, a Zadar specialty, or try some smoked ham (pršut) or cheese (paški sir), both perfect for a snack or to take home.

The market isn't just about food. You'll find vendors selling handmade leather goods, jewelry, and trinkets that are perfect for souvenirs. A visit to the Kali Artisan Center, just a short stroll from the market, will take you deeper into Zadar's artistic heart. This boutique is packed with locally crafted ceramics, paintings, and textiles. The artisan craftsmanship is exceptional, and every piece tells a story of Zadar's rich cultural heritage.

If you're searching for something truly unique, the Škojic Gallery is a hidden gem. This small art gallery offers one-of-a-kind paintings and sculptures by local artists, capturing the essence of Dalmatian life and the surrounding landscapes.

8.2 Dalmatian Specialties to Take Home

Bringing a Taste of Dalmatia Back With You

No trip to Zadar would be complete without bringing home a little something to remember it by, whether it's a bottle of wine or a jar of fig jam, these items encapsulate the flavors of the region.

Start with olive oil. Dalmatia is renowned for its exceptional olive groves, and the olive oil produced here is among the best in the world. You'll find small artisanal producers offering high-quality olive oil infused with herbs like rosemary and lavender. Zadar olive oil often comes in beautifully packaged bottles, making it a perfect gift for friends or a little indulgence for yourself.

Another must-buy is Pag cheese (Paški sir). This sheep's milk cheese, made on the island of Pag, is rich and flavorful, with a sharp tang that reflects the salty air and herbs of the island. You can find it at local delis and markets, and it pairs wonderfully with a bottle of Dalmatian wine.

If you're looking for something sweet, fig jam and cherry preserves are traditional delicacies that often accompany Dalmatian meals. These jams are made with ripe local fruits and have a deep, luscious flavor that's hard to beat. You'll find jars of these treats at both the Green Market and local specialty stores.

For a true local experience, you can pick up a bottle of rakija, a fruit brandy that's commonly consumed as a digestive after meals. It's made from various fruits, but the most popular in Zadar is plum rakija. You can even visit a local distillery to learn how it's made.

8.3 High-End Shopping vs. Budget Finds

Finding the Perfect Balance

Whether you're a luxury shopper or a bargain hunter, Zadar has something for you. The Old Town, with its narrow streets and Venetian-style architecture, is home to a range of stores catering to both high-end shoppers and those on a budget.

High-End Shopping:

For a more luxurious experience, take a stroll along Kalelarga, the main street running through Zadar's Old Town. This pedestrianized area is home to several boutique stores offering Italian fashion, fine jewelry, and designer accessories. Stores like Obala Boutique showcase high-end clothing brands, while Zadar Art Gallery offers exquisite home décor and original artworks from local and international artists.

If you're looking to splurge, Zadar's Luxe Wine Shop offers an impressive selection of premium wines, including rare Croatian varietals from the islands and mainland vineyards.

Budget Finds:

For those of us who prefer to shop without breaking the bank, there are plenty of affordable options. The Green Market is a great place for budget-friendly shopping, especially if you're after local produce, herbs, and handmade crafts.

You can find inexpensive woven baskets, pottery, and handmade soaps at local craft stalls. If you're looking for something more modern and trendy, the City Galleria shopping mall, just outside the Old Town, features international high street brands at reasonable prices. For souvenir hunters, the small shops scattered throughout the Old Town offer affordable options, from keychains and postcards to handmade jewelry and clothing.

8.4 Where to Buy Authentic Croatian Products

Supporting Local Artisans

One of the best ways to support the local economy and take home something truly authentic is by buying products made by Croatian artisans. Many shops in Zadar specialize in locally made goods, and you'll find that these products often carry a deeper cultural significance.

Start at Lokalna Zadruga, a shop that brings together a collection of handmade products made by local artisans. Here, you can find hand-woven textiles, including scarves and tablecloths, as well as ceramic pottery that's hand-painted with traditional Dalmatian patterns. Dalmatian lace, a delicate, intricate art form unique to the region, is also widely available, often as table runners or wall hangings. This lace-making tradition has been passed down for generations and is an excellent souvenir that tells the story of Zadar's past.

For something more practical, leather goods are another must-buy. Zadar is home to several artisan leather shops where you can find handcrafted bags, belts, and wallets made from high-quality Croatian leather. These items make for stylish, long-lasting gifts or keepsakes.

A Piece of Zadar to Take Home

Zadar's charm extends beyond its ancient walls and sparkling waters, it lingers in the small shops, vibrant markets, and artisanal boutiques scattered throughout the city. As you explore, you'll discover the perfect souvenir to remember your trip, whether it's a bottle of locally made olive oil, a piece of handwoven lace, or a jar of sun-ripened fig jam.

The memories you make here are not just about sights and sounds, but also about the flavors, textures, and crafts that tell the story of Zadar's rich cultural heritage. No matter your budget, Zadar offers a treasure trove of unique, locally made goods that you'll cherish long after you leave. So, take your time, explore the shops, and bring home a little piece of this timeless city to share with loved ones, or to keep for yourself.

Chapter 9: Outdoor Adventures & Activities

Zadar, perched along the stunning Adriatic coast, is a paradise for outdoor enthusiasts. Whether you're someone who loves to stroll through ancient streets, hike through breathtaking landscapes, or plunge into the crystal-clear waters, Zadar offers a wealth of experiences to satisfy any adventurer's soul. As I set out to explore this magnificent city, I quickly realized that Zadar isn't just a place to visit, it's a place to experience with all of your senses. In this chapter, I'll share some of the best outdoor activities to help you make the most of your time here, from scenic walks to exhilarating water sports.

9.1 Walking & Hiking Routes

Exploring Zadar on Foot: The Perfect Way to Absorb the City's Beauty

There's something magical about wandering the ancient streets of Zadar on foot. The city's compact size and rich history make it the perfect place to explore on foot, whether you're heading to iconic landmarks or seeking hidden gems off the beaten path.

Start your day with a stroll along Kalelarga, the main pedestrian street that cuts through the heart of the Old Town. As you walk, take in the beautiful Venetian-style buildings that line the street. The cobbled pathways echo with the footsteps of locals and tourists alike, while cafes spill out onto the sidewalks, inviting you to stop and enjoy a coffee or pastry.

For those looking for more active adventures, the Zadar Waterfront Promenade is a great place to enjoy a scenic walk or jog along the sea. From the Sea Organ and Sun Salutation at the city's western tip, you can follow the path that runs along the coastline. The views of the crystal-clear waters and nearby islands are absolutely mesmerizing, particularly as the sun sets over the horizon, casting a golden glow across the sea.

If you're up for a hike, head out of the city and explore the nearby hills for sweeping views of Zadar and the surrounding archipelago. The Vransko Lake Nature Park, just a short drive from the city, offers some of the best hiking routes. Here, you can follow the trails through wetlands and forests, all while spotting local wildlife and enjoying the serenity of the landscape.

9.2 Sea Kayaking, Sailing & Snorkeling

The Adriatic Awaits: Explore Zadar's Waters

Zadar's position on the Adriatic Sea makes it an ideal destination for those who want to explore the water. Whether you prefer the gentle glide of a kayak, the thrill of sailing, or the underwater adventure of snorkeling, Zadar offers endless opportunities for water-based activities.

Sea Kayaking: One of the best ways to explore Zadar's coastline is by sea kayak. Renting a kayak allows you to paddle at your own pace, exploring the hidden coves and secluded beaches that are often missed by tourists. I recommend heading out to Ugljan Island, which is just a short boat ride from Zadar. The island offers calm waters perfect for kayaking, and you'll get to enjoy the island's lush vegetation and rocky coastline from a unique perspective.

Sailing: If you're feeling adventurous and want to get out on the open sea, sailing is a must-try experience in Zadar. The Adriatic coast is dotted with beautiful islands, and a sailing tour will take you to some of the most breathtaking spots. You can opt for a guided sailing trip, where the crew will take care of everything, or rent a small boat if you're an experienced sailor. Dugi Otok, a long and narrow island known for its pristine beaches and picturesque villages, is an excellent destination for a sailing day trip.

Snorkeling: For those who prefer to explore the underwater world, snorkeling is an incredible way to see the vibrant marine life of the Adriatic Sea. The waters around the islands near Zadar are crystal clear, offering excellent visibility. One of my favorite spots for snorkeling is Silba Island, where you can swim alongside schools of fish and discover the underwater world of rocky coves and hidden reefs.

9.3 National Parks & Nature Reserves

Discover Zadar's Natural Wonders

Zadar is surrounded by stunning natural landscapes that are perfect for nature lovers and those looking to escape the hustle and bustle of city life. Within a short distance from the city, you'll find several national parks and nature reserves that are well worth exploring.

Kornati National Park: If there's one place in Zadar that's a must-visit for nature lovers, it's Kornati National Park. Made up of over 140 islands, islets, and reefs, this park is a haven for sailors, hikers, and nature enthusiasts. The islands are rocky and barren but beautiful, with rugged cliffs that drop into the turquoise sea. The park is also home to a variety of wildlife, including sea turtles and rare birds. A boat tour is a great way to explore Kornati, as it gives you access to the islands' most remote and unspoiled areas.

Paklenica National Park: For hikers, Paklenica National Park is a true gem. Located about 45 minutes from Zadar, this park is famous for its dramatic cliffs, deep canyons, and lush forests. There are a variety of trails that cater to different skill levels, ranging from easy walks to more challenging climbs. As you hike through the park, you'll be treated to panoramic views of the surrounding mountains and the Adriatic coastline.

Vransko Lake Nature Park: Just a short drive from Zadar, Vransko Lake offers a peaceful retreat for those looking to connect with nature. The park is home to diverse bird species, making it a popular spot for birdwatching. There are also walking and cycling trails that meander around the lake, offering a tranquil escape from the city.

9.4 Adventure Sports & Thrilling Experiences

For the Thrill-Seeker: Zadar's Action-Packed Adventures

If you're someone who seeks adrenaline-pumping activities, Zadar won't disappoint. From cliff diving to zip-lining, there's no shortage of adventure sports to get your heart racing.

Cliff Diving: The coastline around Zadar is dotted with cliffs, making it an ideal destination for cliff diving. One of the best spots is the small town of Nin, located just outside of Zadar.

The cliffs here rise dramatically from the sea, offering perfect spots for a daring plunge into the crystal-clear waters below. The thrill of jumping into the cool, blue sea is unforgettable, and the views of the surrounding islands are truly spectacular.

Zip-Lining: For a truly exhilarating experience, head to the Paklenica National Park, where you can try your hand at zip-lining. The park offers an exciting zip-lining course that lets you soar above the treetops, taking in stunning views of the canyon below. It's a thrilling way to see the park from a completely different angle.

Cycling: Zadar's scenic coastline and nearby hills make it an excellent destination for cycling. There are plenty of bike rental shops in the city, offering everything from mountain bikes to e-bikes for those who prefer an easier ride. One of the most scenic cycling routes is along the Zadar Riviera, where you'll ride along the coast with views of the sparkling sea and nearby islands.

Outdoor Adventures Await

Zadar's natural beauty is a playground for outdoor adventurers, offering everything from scenic walks through ancient streets to thrilling water sports and hiking trails. Whether you're looking to connect with nature, indulge in adrenaline-pumping activities, or simply enjoy a leisurely walk by the sea, Zadar provides endless opportunities to explore.

The best part? Every adventure brings you closer to the heart and soul of this spectacular city, leaving you with memories that will last a lifetime.

Chapter 10: Dive Into Culture

Zadar is a city that doesn't just live in the present; it thrives in its history and traditions. As a traveler who has ventured through its ancient streets, I've come to realize that the true essence of this city isn't found only in its beautiful landscapes or architectural wonders. It lies in its vibrant cultural fabric, the customs, the art, the music, and the festivals that bring Zadar's identity to life. In this chapter, I'll take you beyond the obvious tourist attractions and into the soul of Zadar's culture, helping you connect with the city on a deeper, more meaningful level.

10.1 Local Customs & Cultural Etiquette

Understanding the Heart of Zadar's People

Croatian culture is deeply rooted in its history, and Zadar, with its rich past, reflects this in its everyday life. As with any destination, respecting local customs and etiquette can help you forge more genuine connections with the people you meet along the way.

Greeting and Politeness: In Zadar, the traditional Croatian greeting is a warm handshake or a simple "Dobar dan" (Good day). If you're invited into someone's home, it's customary to greet with a kiss on both cheeks, especially in more intimate settings.

A polite tone is essential, and people here appreciate when visitors make an effort to learn a few Croatian phrases, even if it's just "Hvala" (Thank you) or "Molim" (Please).

Dining Etiquette: Dining is an integral part of Croatian culture, and Zadar is no exception. When dining in a restaurant, it's customary to wait for the host to initiate the meal. If invited to a local home, it's polite to bring a small gift, such as wine or flowers. Meals are often shared, and in Zadar, the emphasis is on family, friendship, and hospitality. When eating, be sure to keep your hands visible on the table (but not your elbows), and never begin eating until the host says, "Dozvolite" (Let's begin).

Dress Code: While Zadar is a laid-back city, its people still take pride in their appearance, especially when attending social gatherings or dining out. Locals tend to dress smart-casual, even for simple outings. On the beach, however, you'll find a more relaxed dress code, though modesty is still appreciated when leaving the water.

10.2 Traditional Music, Dance & Art

The Rhythms of Zadar: A Symphony of History and Heritage

If you've ever walked through Zadar's narrow cobbled streets, you may have heard the faint strains of music echoing off the ancient walls.

Music here is as old as the city itself, with roots stretching back to Roman times. Traditional music in Zadar blends Slavic influences with Mediterranean rhythms, creating a sound that is uniquely Dalmatian.

Klapa Music: One of the most iconic musical forms in the region is klapa, a style of a cappella singing that originated in Dalmatia. The harmonies of klapa singers, often accompanied by nothing more than the human voice, create a hauntingly beautiful sound. While wandering the streets of Zadar, you might come across a local klapa group performing in a square or during a festival. The music is evocative of the sea and the rugged landscape, and it connects deeply with the local community. If you get the chance to listen to a live performance, it's an experience that stays with you long after the final note fades.

Traditional Dance: Along with music, dance is a vital part of Zadar's cultural heritage. The Linđo is one of the most popular traditional dances in Dalmatia, characterized by fast footwork and a lively rhythm. The dance is often performed during festivals and public celebrations, and locals take great pride in passing the tradition down through generations. Watching a Linđo performance is an energizing experience, as dancers move with precision and enthusiasm, bringing the history of the region to life through their steps.

Art Scene: Zadar's artistic legacy is equally rich. The city is home to numerous galleries and studios, where both traditional and contemporary art are celebrated. The Zadar City Museum and the Museum of Ancient Glass showcase art and artifacts that span the city's long history, offering visitors a glimpse into the past. For those interested in modern art, Zadar is also home to a thriving scene of contemporary galleries and public art installations, such as the Sea Organ, which is not only an architectural wonder but also a piece of art that interacts with the natural environment.

10.3 Festivals & Local Celebrations

A Celebration of Life: Zadar's Festivals Throughout the Year

One of the best ways to truly experience the heart and soul of Zadar is by attending one of its vibrant festivals. These events are a reflection of the city's rich history and cultural diversity, offering a lively mix of music, dance, food, and local traditions.

The Zadar Summer Festival is one of the city's most famous cultural events. Held every year in July and August, this festival showcases everything from opera and classical music to theater and contemporary dance. The performances take place in some of Zadar's most picturesque locations, such as the Roman Forum and the St. Donatus Church, where the ancient surroundings enhance the beauty of the cultural expressions.

For a more intimate cultural experience, don't miss the Zadar International Film Festival, which celebrates independent cinema from around the world. Held in late autumn, this festival draws filmmakers and film lovers to Zadar to enjoy screenings of documentaries, shorts, and feature films in various languages. It's an opportunity to experience the city's modern cultural side while mingling with creatives and enjoying the laid-back atmosphere.

Local Wine & Food Festivals are also an integral part of Zadar's culture. The Zadar Wine Festival, held in spring, offers a delightful way to explore Croatian wine and culinary traditions. Local vineyards open their doors to visitors, offering tastings of fine wines paired with Dalmatian delicacies. During these festivals, you can also learn about traditional winemaking methods that have been passed down through generations.

10.4 Religious and Historic Heritage

The Spiritual Heart of Zadar

Zadar is not just a cultural hub; it's also a city of deep spiritual significance. Its religious heritage, dating back over a thousand years, is evident in its many churches, monasteries, and historical landmarks.

St. Donatus Church is one of the most famous landmarks in Zadar, a striking example of early Christian architecture. Built in the 9th century, the church's circular design and Romanesque architecture offer a glimpse into the city's Byzantine past. The church stands as a testament to the city's historical religious influence and is still an active site for religious ceremonies today.

The Cathedral of St. Anastasia, located in the heart of the city, is another must-see for those interested in Zadar's spiritual history. It's the largest church in Dalmatia and boasts beautiful Romanesque and Byzantine architecture. Inside, you'll find stunning mosaics, frescoes, and the tomb of St. Anastasia, the city's patron saint.

Throughout Zadar, the influence of the Catholic Church is evident in local traditions and festivals, many of which are tied to religious holidays and saints' days. These celebrations, deeply rooted in the local community, offer visitors a unique chance to experience the city's spiritual customs firsthand.

Immersing Yourself in Zadar's Culture

Zadar's culture is rich, diverse, and woven deeply into the city's identity. From the music that echoes through its ancient streets to the festivals that bring it to life, every aspect of this city invites you to dive deeper and connect with its history.

Whether you're exploring local customs, experiencing the rhythms of traditional music, or witnessing the grandeur of its religious heritage, Zadar offers an unforgettable cultural journey. So, step into the heart of the city, let its history envelop you, and experience the true soul of Zadar.

Chapter 11: Seasonal Travel Guide

Zadar is one of those rare places that feels timeless, yet it transforms with each season. Whether you're looking for the vibrancy of summer, the quiet charm of autumn, or the peaceful allure of winter, Zadar offers something special for every type of traveler, no matter when you visit. Over the years, I've come to appreciate how the city's personality shifts with the seasons. In this chapter, I'll take you through Zadar's four seasons, providing insider tips, the best events to attend, and recommendations to help you experience the destination at its best, no matter the time of year.

11.1 Spring in Zadar: Events, Wildflowers, and Quiet Exploration

Spring in Zadar is nothing short of magical. As the city shakes off the chill of winter, a fresh energy fills the air. The streets, once quieter, now start to buzz with the vibrancy of locals enjoying the warmer weather. Spring is perfect for those who want to experience Zadar in a more peaceful light, with fewer tourists and a city still slowly coming alive.

Events & Festivals: One of the highlights of spring is the Zadar Music Festival, which takes place in late April and early May. The festival celebrates classical music with performances in stunning venues like the St. Donatus Church and Zadar's Roman Forum. It's a great way to experience Zadar's musical heritage in a truly historic setting. If you're a fan of culture, the Zadar Spring Festival offers a mix of theater, art exhibitions, and local performances.

Wildflowers & Outdoor Exploration: Spring is also the perfect time to explore the nature around Zadar, with wildflowers dotting the landscape. You'll find the Paklenica National Park just a short drive from the city, where hiking paths lined with vibrant blooms await. For something a little quieter, the Zadar Hinterland is a wonderful option, with rolling hills and charming stone villages, offering an authentic slice of Dalmatian life.

Quiet Corners & Historical Exploration: If you prefer a more serene experience, spring in Zadar provides a peaceful environment for exploring the city's historical landmarks without the crowds. Walk along the ancient City Walls, visit the Roman Forum, or simply sit by the Sea Organ, listening to the harmonious sound of the waves interacting with the pipes, while soaking in the gentle warmth of the spring sun.

11.2 Summer: Beach Life, Night Markets, and Concerts

Summer is when Zadar truly comes alive. The city's beaches, already stunning, take on a whole new vibe as the sun blazes down and the sea sparkles under the clear blue sky. It's a time for lounging on the beach, taking in the warm Mediterranean breeze, and indulging in the lively atmosphere that makes Zadar one of the most sought-after destinations in Croatia.

Beach Life: Whether you're into lounging or diving into the crystal-clear waters, Zadar's beaches offer something for everyone. Kolovare Beach, located close to the city center, is perfect for those who prefer easy access to cafes and restaurants. For a more secluded experience, Sakarun Beach on the island of Dugi Otok is famous for its soft white sand and turquoise waters. Bring a good book, your sunhat, and prepare to spend a few lazy hours soaking up the sun.

Night Markets & Local Vibes: As the sun sets, the city transforms into a vibrant hub of activity. The Zadar Night Market, held in the evenings, is the perfect place to wander, try local specialties, and immerse yourself in the local culture. The market is filled with fresh produce, artisanal goods, and live music that creates an electric atmosphere as you shop for unique souvenirs or grab a snack.

It's an opportunity to mingle with locals and other travelers while enjoying the warm summer nights.

Concerts & Nightlife: Summer in Zadar also means music. Zadar is home to numerous outdoor concerts, including live jazz performances and rock festivals that take place throughout the city. Head to the City's Forum or the outdoor amphitheater for some of the best open-air concerts, where the backdrop of the sea only adds to the ambiance. Zadar's nightlife, especially along the waterfront, comes alive with beach bars, cocktail lounges, and nightclubs where you can dance until the early hours of the morning.

11.3 Autumn: Harvests, Wine Tours, and Mild Weather

Autumn is one of my personal favorite times to visit Zadar. The city becomes a tranquil haven, with warm temperatures and fewer crowds. The summer rush is over, and the streets feel less hectic, allowing for a more relaxed and intimate experience. The mild weather and beautiful autumnal hues make Zadar feel like a hidden gem.

Harvest & Culinary Delights: Autumn in Zadar is synonymous with the harvest season. You'll find local markets brimming with fresh figs, grapes, olives, and truffles.

It's the perfect time to explore Dalmatian cuisine, especially the dishes that are inspired by seasonal ingredients. You must try pašticada (a slow-cooked beef stew) or peka (a traditional dish of meat and vegetables cooked under a bell-like lid). Local restaurants serve these hearty dishes alongside fresh olive oil, and paired with a glass of local wine, they make for an unforgettable meal.

Wine Tours: Zadar is in the heart of Croatia's wine country, and autumn is the best time to explore the region's vineyards. The Zadar Wine Festival, usually held in October, is a great way to taste a variety of wines, meet the winemakers, and learn about the history of Croatian viticulture. You can also take a day trip to nearby Benkovac or Bibich Winery, where you can tour the vineyards and taste the wine while enjoying the stunning views of the surrounding hills and coastline.

Mild Weather for Exploration: Autumn is a perfect time to explore Zadar's outdoor attractions without the summer heat. Take a hike in Vransko Lake Nature Park, a haven for birdwatchers, or explore the Paklenica National Park, where the trails are not as crowded but still offer breathtaking views of the rugged landscapes.

11.4 Winter: Quiet Retreats, Holiday Spirit, and Off-Season Tips

While winter in Zadar is quieter, it offers a serene escape that's perfect for travelers seeking peace and solitude. The chilly weather gives the city a completely different, almost ethereal quality, and there's a charm to wandering the streets with fewer crowds and the soft glow of winter lights reflecting off the stone buildings.

Quiet Retreats & Peaceful Exploration: Winter is the ideal time for those looking to retreat into the tranquility of Zadar. The city's historical landmarks, such as the St. Donatus Church and Zadar Archaeological Museum, are even more atmospheric in the winter months, where the absence of large crowds gives you time to truly absorb the significance of these ancient sites. Take a stroll along the Sea Organ at sunset, and you'll feel like you have the city all to yourself, the waves creating a peaceful soundtrack as you admire the view.

Holiday Spirit & Christmas Markets: During the festive season, Zadar transforms into a winter wonderland. The Christmas Market fills Narodni Trg (People's Square) with local vendors selling handmade crafts, ornaments, and delicious food. You can sample kulen (spicy sausage) or enjoy a warm cup of mulled wine while soaking in the holiday atmosphere.

The city lights up with decorations, and if you're lucky, you might even experience a local Christmas concert or holiday performance at the Zadar Theatre.

Off-Season Travel Tips: Traveling in the off-season allows you to enjoy Zadar at a slower pace. Many of the restaurants and accommodations offer off-season deals, which means you can enjoy luxury at a fraction of the price. Be sure to dress warmly, as the weather can be crisp, but with the right layers, you can still enjoy outdoor exploration. This is also a great time to explore the quieter parts of the city and discover hidden gems that may be overlooked during peak tourist seasons.

Zadar Through the Seasons

Zadar's charm lies in its ability to offer something different in every season. Whether you're drawn to the lively buzz of summer, the peaceful charm of winter, the harvest-time feasts of autumn, or the blooming beauty of spring, the city never fails to provide a fulfilling and memorable experience. So, whatever time of year you decide to visit, Zadar will undoubtedly leave an imprint on your heart, making it a destination to return to again and again.

Chapter 12: Ready-Made Itineraries

Zadar, Croatia, is a city where ancient history meets stunning nature and modern-day vibrancy. If you're planning to visit, you may find yourself overwhelmed by all the possibilities. Whether you have just a day to spare or an entire week to explore, Zadar has a way of revealing its best side to every type of traveler. In this chapter, I'll walk you through several tailor-made itineraries that suit a variety of interests, from a whirlwind highlights tour to a relaxing romantic escape. These itineraries are designed to help you make the most of your time, ensuring you don't miss the city's must-sees while also uncovering hidden gems along the way.

12.1 One Day in Zadar: Highlights Tour

If you have just a day in Zadar, you'll want to hit the ground running. The key to a perfect one-day itinerary is to mix the most iconic sights with a few moments of pure Zadar magic.

Morning: Start your day early by heading to The Sea Organ at sunrise. The soft, melodic sounds created by the waves interacting with the organ pipes will set the tone for your day.

Just next door, don't miss the Greeting to the Sun installation, a stunning display of solar-powered light panels that comes alive with color as the sun rises. After soaking in the serenity, take a short stroll to Zadar's Roman Forum and the St. Donatus Church, one of Croatia's best-preserved medieval buildings. The Roman ruins here offer a fascinating glimpse into the past and set the stage for the city's deep historical roots.

Midday: After immersing yourself in Zadar's past, head to the Zadar Old Town for lunch at a local restaurant. I recommend Konoba Skoblar, a family-owned place where you can enjoy delicious Dalmatian seafood and sample local specialties like black risotto or grilled sardines. After lunch, wander the cobbled streets of the Old Town, popping into boutique shops or stopping at one of the cafés for an afternoon coffee.

Afternoon: Make your way to St. Anastasia's Cathedral, the largest in Dalmatia, and climb the bell tower for panoramic views of Zadar and the surrounding islands. Afterward, head over to Veli Varos, a peaceful neighborhood filled with charming streets and pastel-colored buildings, perfect for a leisurely walk. End your day with a relaxing moment by the City Walls, you'll get a beautiful view of the sea, especially at sunset, before finishing up with a dinner at one of Zadar's fantastic seafood restaurants.

12.2 Three-Day City Experience

With three days in Zadar, you can dig deeper into its culture, history, and natural beauty. Here's how to enjoy the best of both the city and its surrounding regions.

Day 1: Historic Core & Iconic Landmarks

Start your adventure in the Old Town, just as in the one-day itinerary, but allow yourself more time to appreciate the charm of the Roman Forum and the St. Donatus Church. Explore the Zadar Archaeological Museum to learn about the city's layered past, and don't miss the nearby Museum of Ancient Glass, where you can admire collections of Roman and early Christian glass.

In the afternoon, visit the Zadar Marina and enjoy a walk along the water to the Lighthouse for a lovely sea breeze. For dinner, dine at Restaurant 2Ribara for a local culinary experience.

Day 2: Nature & Day Trips

Take a day trip to Kornati National Park, an archipelago known for its rugged beauty and crystal-clear waters. You can book a boat tour from Zadar's harbor to explore the stunning islands, ideal for swimming, hiking, or simply relaxing on quiet beaches. On your return, stop by the Zadar Fish Market, where you can purchase fresh local seafood or sample fresh oysters from the nearby islands.

Day 3: Sea & Sun

Spend your final day embracing Zadar's incredible coastline. Visit Kolovare Beach for a relaxing swim or head out to Sakarun Beach on the island of Dugi Otok for a tranquil, picturesque setting. If you're in the mood for adventure, rent a kayak or take a snorkeling tour to explore the vibrant marine life. For your evening, enjoy a sunset dinner at one of the seaside restaurants, like Pet Bunara, which offers a fresh take on Dalmatian cuisine.

12.3 A Full Week in Zadar & Surroundings

For a more leisurely pace, a full week allows you to explore Zadar and the surrounding areas in greater depth. This itinerary balances city exploration, nature, and day trips.

Day 1-3: Zadar Essentials

Spend your first three days as described in the Three-Day City Experience. Enjoy the historical sites, indulge in delicious local food, and explore the natural beauty of the area with a day trip to Kornati National Park. By now, you'll have gotten a feel for Zadar's rhythm, with ample time to enjoy the restaurants, beaches, and charming streets without rushing.

Day 4: Nin & Zaton

Take a short drive to Nin, a quaint town known for its Roman ruins, sandy beaches, and saltworks. Visit the Church of St. Nicholas and enjoy a walk along the town's scenic streets. In the afternoon, head to Zaton, a coastal resort area, for a relaxing time on the beach or a visit to the local vineyards. A wine-tasting tour here is an excellent way to unwind.

Day 5: Paklenica National Park

Devote an entire day to Paklenica National Park. The park is a haven for nature lovers and adventure seekers, with hiking trails that offer panoramic views of the Velebit Mountains. Even if you're not a seasoned hiker, there are plenty of gentle walks, and the rich biodiversity of the park is fascinating. After a day of outdoor activities, head back to Zadar for a well-earned dinner.

Day 6: Dugi Otok & Telascica

A boat trip to Dugi Otok is a must for those who want to experience a more untouched side of the Zadar Archipelago. On the island, you'll find the Telascica Nature Park, a tranquil spot where you can swim in calm waters and hike the cliffs for stunning views of the Adriatic.

Day 7: Relax and Indulge

For your final day, take it easy. Spend a lazy morning exploring Zadar's backstreets and enjoying a slow brunch at one of the city's many excellent cafés. In the afternoon, pamper yourself with a spa day at a luxury hotel or relax by the beach with a book. Finish your week with a sunset dinner at The Landing, a fine dining experience that showcases the best of Dalmatian cuisine.

12.4 Family-Focused Adventures

Zadar is an excellent destination for families, offering a range of activities that cater to all ages.

- **Sea Organ & Greeting to the Sun**: The kids will love the mesmerizing sounds of the Sea Organ and the light show at Greeting to the Sun.

- **Zadar Aquarium**: Located near the city center, the aquarium offers a great introduction to marine life and is ideal for younger children.

- **Beaches & Water Sports**: Spend a day at Kolovare Beach, where kids can play on the shore while parents relax. Rent a pedal boat or take a family-friendly kayak tour for an adventure on the water.

12.5 Couples' Romantic Escape

For couples seeking romance, Zadar offers a perfect balance of intimate moments and beautiful landscapes.

- **Sunset Stroll**: Take a romantic walk along the city's ancient walls at sunset, hand-in-hand as the sky turns vibrant shades of orange and pink.

- **Private Boat Trip**: Charter a private boat for a romantic day trip to the nearby islands. Swim, snorkel, or simply relax on the deck with a glass of wine in hand.

- **Fine Dining**: For a special dinner, head to Restaurant Kornat, where you can enjoy exquisite seafood while overlooking the beautiful harbor.

12.6 Budget Explorer's Route

Zadar is incredibly affordable for travelers on a budget. Here's how to make the most of your time without breaking the bank.

- **Free Activities**: Many of Zadar's main attractions, like the Sea Organ and Greeting to the Sun, are completely free to visit. Exploring the city's Old Town and the city walls won't cost a dime.

- **Affordable Dining**: Try local konobas (taverns) for inexpensive yet delicious Dalmatian meals. The Riva promenade has several affordable options with stunning views.

12.7 Luxury & VIP Indulgence

For those seeking luxury, Zadar has plenty to offer, from high-end dining to indulgent experiences.

- **Luxury Dining**: Treat yourself to a meal at Restaurant 2Ribara, known for its fresh seafood and sophisticated atmosphere.

- **Private Yacht Tour**: Charter a private yacht for a luxurious cruise around the islands, complete with a gourmet lunch prepared on board.

- **Exclusive Spas**: Spend a day pampering yourself at one of the luxury hotels in Zadar, where you can enjoy world-class spa services, private beach access, and top-tier accommodations.

Tailor Your Zadar Experience

Zadar's versatility as a destination ensures there's an itinerary for every kind of traveler.

Whether you're here for a quick stop or an extended exploration, you'll find the perfect balance of history, nature, adventure, and relaxation. Enjoy your trip to Zadar, and let it leave you with memories that will last a lifetime.

Chapter 13: Best Day Trips from Zadar

Zadar is a gem of a city, brimming with history, culture, and stunning natural beauty. But what makes this Croatian destination truly unforgettable is its proximity to a myriad of exceptional day-trip options. Whether you're a history buff, nature lover, or beach enthusiast, the surrounding areas offer plenty of opportunities for exploration. As someone who's explored every corner of Zadar and its environs, I've curated some of the best day trips that will allow you to experience the essence of Dalmatia in all its glory.

So pack your bags (or simply hop on a bus or boat) and get ready to explore these magnificent day trips from Zadar.

13.1 Nin & Pag Island

Distance from Zadar: 20 minutes by car to Nin, 1 hour to Pag Island

If you're looking for a day trip that combines history, stunning beaches, and a taste of the local way of life, a visit to Nin and Pag Island is essential.

Nin is often overlooked by tourists, but it's a place brimming with charm and significance. The town's Romanesque churches, like St. Nicholas Church, are steeped in history, and the salt pans that stretch across the landscape offer a tranquil and picturesque scene. One of the most captivating sites is The Church of the Holy Cross, known as the "smallest cathedral in the world," standing proudly in the heart of Nin. It's an ideal spot for a quiet moment of reflection.

After soaking in the town's history, head over to Pag Island. The island is famous for its unique moon-like landscape and is a haven for food lovers. The island's sheep cheese, known as Paški sir, is legendary. Stop by one of the local shops or farms to taste it fresh. Pag's coastline is also dotted with stunning beaches, such as Zrće Beach, a lively destination in summer for party-goers, and Ručica Beach, which is more peaceful and perfect for a swim.

Tip: Rent a car to explore the island at your own pace, and be sure to stop at Novalja for a relaxing meal overlooking the sea.

13.2 Kornati National Park

Distance from Zadar: 1.5 hours by boat

For those who want to experience Croatia's stunning coastline at its most rugged and untouched, Kornati National Park is the place to be.

This archipelago, comprising nearly 150 islands, is a paradise for nature lovers, photographers, and those who simply want to disconnect from the hustle and bustle.

A boat trip from Zadar to Kornati will give you panoramic views of the Adriatic Sea and its sapphire-blue waters, dotted with small, rocky islands that look almost otherworldly. You can swim, snorkel, or simply relax on the deck as you cruise between the islands. One of the highlights is Telašćica Bay, a protected natural harbor with calm waters and dramatic cliffs that plunge into the sea.

Tip: If you're into hiking, several trails on the islands will lead you to panoramic viewpoints. For those interested in local wildlife, look out for bald eagles and cormorants that call these islands home.

A trip to Kornati feels like stepping into a different world, a peaceful, unspoiled landscape that's perfect for a day of relaxation and exploration.

13.3 Plitvice Lakes National Park

Distance from Zadar: 1.5 to 2 hours by car

One of Croatia's most iconic natural wonders, Plitvice Lakes National Park, is a must-see for anyone with a love of nature.

This UNESCO World Heritage site is a vast network of 16 terraced lakes connected by waterfalls and surrounded by dense forests. The cascading waters, vibrant blue and turquoise hues, and abundant wildlife make it a photographer's dream.

Start your day early to maximize your time in this natural paradise. As you wander along the well-maintained wooden pathways that snake through the park, the sound of water rushing over the waterfalls will fill the air, creating a tranquil atmosphere. Veliki Slap, the park's largest waterfall, is a must-see, standing an impressive 78 meters tall.

Tip: Wear comfortable shoes and bring water, there are plenty of walking trails, and you'll want to explore as much as possible. It's also a good idea to visit during the shoulder seasons, in late spring or early autumn, to avoid the summer crowds.

Plitvice is a peaceful, awe-inspiring destination that makes you feel like you've stepped into a fairy tale. It's an adventure that combines both breathtaking beauty and tranquility.

13.4 Šibenik, Krka Waterfalls & More Coastal Gems

Distance from Zadar: 1.5 hours by car to Šibenik, 30 minutes to Krka Waterfalls

If you're seeking a blend of history, nature, and seaside charm, a day trip to Šibenik and the nearby Krka Waterfalls should be at the top of your list.

Šibenik is a historic city perched along the coast, and its most iconic landmark is the St. James Cathedral, a UNESCO World Heritage site. It's beautiful Renaissance architecture and stone-carved details are impressive, but it's also the view from the cathedral's square that steals the show, overlooking the sparkling blue waters of the Adriatic.

After exploring the city, take a short drive to Krka National Park, home to the famous Krka Waterfalls. The park features a series of waterfalls and lakes, with Skradinski Buk being the largest and most famous. Take a boat ride along the river, hike the trails, or simply bask in the natural beauty. You can even swim near the base of the waterfalls during the summer months, which adds an element of fun to the visit.

Tip: Combine your visit to Krka with a trip to Roski Slap, another lesser-known waterfall in the park. It's quieter and less touristy but equally beautiful.

For a true coastal adventure, make sure to explore the small towns along the way, like Vodice, where you can enjoy fresh seafood while overlooking the Adriatic.

13.5 Wine Country and Countryside Escapes

Distance from Zadar: 1 hour by car

For those looking to explore the picturesque Dalmatian countryside and taste some incredible local wines, a day trip to wine country is an unforgettable experience. Just a short drive from Zadar, you'll find the regions of Benkovac and Paklenica, perfect for wine lovers and those wanting to escape the crowds.

Here, the local vineyards produce some of the best wines in Croatia, particularly the indigenous varieties of Plavac Mali and Pošip. Take a tour through the vineyards and learn about the wine-making process, followed by a tasting session where you can savor the rich, full-bodied flavors of Dalmatia.

Tip: Pair your wine tasting with a visit to a traditional Konoba (tavern), where you can enjoy freshly made pasticada (a slow-cooked beef stew) or peka (meat or seafood cooked under a bell-shaped lid), and enjoy the true flavors of the region.

Make the Most of Your Zadar Experience

With so many incredible day trips from Zadar, you'll never run out of things to explore. Whether you're hiking through lush national parks, diving into the crystal-clear waters of the Adriatic, or indulging in delicious local food and wine, each day brings something new and exciting. And as you venture outside Zadar, you'll find a peaceful, beautiful landscape that offers a perfect balance of adventure and relaxation. So take the time to explore, discover new corners of Dalmatia, and make memories that will last long after your trip has ended.

Chapter 14: Nightlife & Evening Delights

Zadar, a city bathed in history, is equally alive when the sun sets, offering a captivating and diverse array of experiences. From leisurely sunset strolls to lively club nights and cultural events, Zadar's nightlife reflects the city's rich heritage while embracing the energy of modernity. If you're a traveler who wants to explore the evening side of this charming coastal gem, this chapter will be your ultimate guide to discovering the best spots for a night out. Join me as we explore everything from peaceful beach lounges to the pulse of the city's vibrant nightlife.

14.1 Sunset Spots & Beach Lounges

There's something almost magical about watching the sun dip below the horizon in Zadar. The city's coastal location offers an abundance of sunset spots, each with its own character, where the sky burns with hues of orange and pink, reflecting on the serene waters of the Adriatic.

One of the most iconic spots to catch the sunset is the Sea Organ (Morske Orgulje) at the Zadar waterfront. Located along the western edge of the Old Town, this architectural marvel is not just a place to watch the sunset but also an experience in itself.

The Sea Organ uses the power of the waves to produce harmonious sounds, creating an atmosphere that perfectly complements the breathtaking view. Sitting on the steps as the sun sets and the ocean sings is one of Zadar's most poetic and peaceful experiences.

For a more relaxed atmosphere, head to Kolovare Beach. This tranquil beach is an ideal place to enjoy a sunset with a cocktail in hand, while the gentle waves lap at the shore. You'll often find locals and visitors alike soaking up the evening sun, unwinding after a day of exploring. The nearby beach bars, like Beach Bar "Zadar", offer a range of refreshing drinks and cocktails, perfect for enjoying the sunset with friends or a special someone.

For something a little more sophisticated, head to the luxury bar at Hotel Bastion. Perched above the old town, it provides stunning panoramic views of the city's rooftops and the shimmering sea beyond. With expertly crafted cocktails and a cozy yet upscale ambiance, it's the perfect place to watch the sun sink behind the horizon in style.

Tip: To fully embrace Zadar's laid-back coastal vibe, plan to arrive at your sunset spot a little earlier than usual, and settle in with a cold drink, this way, you can watch the city slowly transition from day to night, experiencing the colors and sounds of Zadar at its most beautiful.

14.2 Bars, Clubs & Live Music Venues

As the sun sets and the stars begin to twinkle above, Zadar's nightlife begins to pulse with life. Whether you're looking to sip cocktails on a terrace, listen to live music, or dance the night away, there's a venue for every type of night owl.

For a true taste of Zadar's social scene, begin your evening in the Old Town. Wander through its narrow, cobbled streets and you'll come across charming bars tucked away in atmospheric corners. Arsenal is one such venue, a historical building turned into a hip spot for both drinks and live music. Located just off the main square, this bar regularly hosts events featuring local bands and DJs, offering a cool mix of modern beats and cultural vibrancy. The acoustics of the space, combined with the laid-back, local crowd, make it a perfect place to enjoy Zadar's music scene.

Another bar that exudes a lively, fun atmosphere is The Garden Lounge, located on the Zadar waterfront. This open-air bar is an essential stop for cocktail lovers, serving up refreshing drinks while overlooking the stunning sea and the nearby islands. The relaxed vibe, combined with breathtaking views, makes it a favorite for watching the evening crowd go by. The Garden Lounge often features DJs and live performances, so be prepared for a spontaneous dance party by the sea.

For those seeking something more energetic, Shakers Bar is the place to be. Located near the city's bustling center, Shakers offers a high-energy nightlife experience with expertly crafted cocktails and an upbeat atmosphere. The bar attracts a mix of locals and tourists, and it's often filled with people enjoying the music and dancing into the early hours of the morning.

When it comes to clubs, the Lighthouse Club stands out. Situated along the waterfront, this is Zadar's prime nightlife venue for dancing until the early hours. Expect house and electronic music as the DJ pumps out beats, keeping the crowd moving. The stunning sea views add an extra layer of magic to the clubbing experience, making it an unforgettable night out.

Tip: If you're interested in live music, keep an eye on Zadar's event calendar. Throughout the year, the city hosts a variety of live performances, from classical music at the City Theatre to rock concerts in outdoor venues.

14.3 Cultural Nights: Theater, Film, and Local Events

While Zadar's bars and clubs provide plenty of excitement, the city also offers a more refined side to its nightlife, where you can immerse yourself in its cultural richness. For those who want to experience the city's cultural scene after hours, Zadar won't disappoint.

One of the standout cultural venues is the Zadar National Theatre, which offers an eclectic mix of performances throughout the year, from classical theater to contemporary plays. The theater is housed in a beautiful 19th-century building, and it's a wonderful spot to enjoy an evening of artistic expression. If you're lucky, you might catch a local production or a visiting company putting on a play that highlights Croatia's rich dramatic heritage.

For film lovers, the Zadar Film Festival is a must-see event. Held annually, this festival brings together filmmakers from all over the world to showcase their work. You can enjoy a wide range of screenings, from indie films to documentaries, often set in the stunning open-air venues near the city's ancient walls. Watching a film here under the stars, surrounded by history, adds a touch of magic to the experience.

Zadar's local festivals also offer unique cultural experiences that bring the city to life in the evenings. Zadar Summer Theatre, Zadar Music Biennale, and Vallis Aurea Music Festival are just a few examples of the city's cultural offerings. Whether it's a classical concert in one of Zadar's ancient churches or a jazz performance on a scenic rooftop, these festivals allow you to experience the artistic soul of Zadar.

Tip: If you're visiting during the summer months, check the schedule for local festivals or performances before you arrive. You can often find performances in intimate settings, such as the Roman Forum or the Church of St. Donatus, where the acoustics and ambiance will add depth to the experience.

Zadar After Dark

As night falls over Zadar, the city unveils a completely different side of itself, one filled with rich cultural experiences, exciting nightlife, and stunning coastal views. Whether you're enjoying a peaceful sunset on the waterfront, sipping cocktails at a beach bar, dancing to electronic beats in a club, or attending a cultural event, Zadar has something for every type of evening adventurer.

Each evening in Zadar is an invitation to dive deeper into the city's vibrant and diverse nightlife. From the most laid-back beach lounges to the high-energy pulse of the clubs, and from intimate cultural events to local festivals, the city offers endless possibilities for memorable nights out. It's a place where the old world meets the new, where history and modernity coexist, and where each evening invites you to experience the magic of this beautiful Adriatic city.

As you venture through Zadar after dark, let the city's energy and charm sweep you away, creating unforgettable memories to carry with you long after the night ends.

Chapter 15: Travel Tips & Safety Essentials

When embarking on a journey to a place as rich in history and beauty as Zadar, it's important to be well-prepared. Whether you're a seasoned traveler or a first-time visitor, understanding the local customs, safety essentials, and useful tools can enhance your experience and ensure your trip is smooth and stress-free. In this chapter, I'll share valuable tips and insights that will help you navigate Zadar like a local, stay safe, and make the most of your time in this enchanting city.

15.1 Health, Safety & Local Laws

Zadar is a relatively safe destination, and health services in Croatia are of a high standard. However, it's always wise to be aware of a few important safety and health considerations before you head out.

Health Care in Zadar

In case you need medical attention, Zadar has modern healthcare facilities, including the Zadar General Hospital, which provides a full range of services, from emergency care to routine medical treatments. Pharmacies are widely available throughout the city, and many offer over-the-counter medications and advice in English.

You'll find them open during regular hours, with some providing after-hours services, especially in the summer months when tourist numbers are at their peak.

Travel Insurance

It's highly recommended to travel with health insurance that covers medical emergencies abroad, including repatriation. This will provide peace of mind in case of unexpected illness or accidents. Many Croatian medical facilities accept EU health cards, but it's worth checking the specifics of your insurance policy.

Local Laws

Croatia is a country that respects order and civility, so it's important to be aware of and respect local laws. Drinking alcohol in public places is generally allowed, but some areas, particularly near schools and churches, may have restrictions. Smoking is prohibited in indoor public spaces, including restaurants and cafes, but many outdoor spaces do have designated smoking areas.

It's also important to note that Croatia follows strict laws on drug use. Possession of illegal substances can lead to serious legal consequences, and the penalties are steep. Always err on the side of caution when it comes to drugs, and remember that the legal drinking age is 18.

Personal Safety

Zadar is known for being a safe city for tourists. Violent crime is extremely rare, but like any popular destination, it's important to stay vigilant, especially in crowded places like markets or tourist-heavy spots. Keep an eye on your belongings, particularly when visiting popular areas like the Roman Forum or the Sea Organ, as pickpockets can sometimes operate in these locations.

Tip: Carry a photocopy of your passport, medical insurance details, and emergency contacts with you in case you lose your wallet or need assistance. It's always a good idea to store your documents in a secure location, like a hotel safe.

15.2 Scams to Avoid & How to Stay Safe

As with any tourist destination, Zadar is not immune to a few common scams, but with a little awareness, you can easily avoid them.

Taxi Scams

In Zadar, taxis are generally safe and reliable, but occasionally, unscrupulous drivers may try to overcharge tourists. Always agree on the fare before entering the taxi or, better yet, use ride-sharing services like Uber or Bolt, which are widely available in the city. These services provide clear pricing, making it easier to avoid any unexpected costs.

Restaurant Scams

While dining in Zadar is an absolute delight, it's important to be cautious of restaurants that might try to take advantage of tourists. Watch out for menus without prices or "hidden charges" added to your bill. Always check the menu prices before ordering, and be aware of any service fees that may be included. If you're uncertain, ask the waiter to clarify before committing.

Street Vendors & Souvenir Shops

Be cautious when purchasing souvenirs from street vendors or small shops, especially those in high-traffic tourist areas. Some vendors may offer items at inflated prices, so it's always a good idea to compare prices between a few shops. Bargaining is not common practice in Croatia, but if you feel the price is too high, try politely negotiating.

Tip: Stick to well-established shops or markets, like the Zadar City Market, which offers a wide selection of authentic, high-quality local products.

General Safety Tip

Always trust your instincts. If something feels off or too good to be true, it's usually best to walk away. Zadar's atmosphere is generally welcoming, but like any destination, being aware of your surroundings and avoiding isolated areas late at night is key to staying safe.

15.3 Emergency Contacts & Services

In case of an emergency, it's good to know who to contact and where to turn for help. Below is a list of essential emergency contacts and services in Zadar:

Emergency Numbers

- **General Emergency (Police, Fire, Ambulance): 112**

  o   This is the number to dial for any type of emergency, whether it's medical, fire, or police-related.

- **Police (Non-Emergency): 092**

- **Ambulance: 194**

- **Zadar General Hospital: +385 23 391 111**

Embassy & Consulate Information

In case of a lost passport, legal trouble, or other serious issues, it's essential to know where your embassy or consulate is located. The U.S. Embassy in Zagreb can assist American citizens, and the British Embassy offers similar support for UK nationals.

Tip: If you need urgent medical assistance, Zadar's General Hospital is your first stop. However, if you're staying in a hotel, always check with the reception as they can help arrange medical services quickly.

Pharmacies

There are plenty of pharmacies in Zadar, and many are open until late in the evening. If you need medical supplies, common over-the-counter medications, or need to consult with a pharmacist, you'll have no trouble finding one. If you need a pharmacy in the middle of the night, ask your hotel for directions to the nearest 24-hour pharmacy.

15.4 Useful Apps & Traveler Tools

Modern technology can be a traveler's best friend, especially when navigating a new city. Here are some apps and tools that can make your time in Zadar easier and more enjoyable.

Google Maps

This is your go-to app for navigating the city, finding hidden gems, and locating public transportation stops. It's incredibly useful when you want to wander through Zadar's winding streets, as it helps you stay oriented even in the maze-like Old Town.

Uber or Bolt

As mentioned earlier, Uber and Bolt are popular and reliable ride-sharing services in Zadar, offering convenient transportation options for getting around town. These apps are also great for avoiding the hassle of negotiating fares with taxi drivers.

Zadar City Guide Apps

Several apps are dedicated to Zadar, offering detailed city maps, lists of attractions, restaurant recommendations, and even event schedules. Zadar Travel Guide and TripAdvisor are both excellent choices for discovering hidden gems, checking reviews, and finding the best spots for food and entertainment.

Currency Converter

While Croatia uses the kuna as currency, many tourists are more familiar with the euro. A currency converter app can help you keep track of exchange rates and ensure you're not caught off guard when paying for meals or souvenirs.

Language Translation Apps

While many people in Zadar speak English, having a translation app (like Google Translate) can be handy, especially in rural areas or smaller shops where English might not be as commonly spoken.

Tip: Download these apps before you leave home to save yourself time and data charges once you're in Zadar. Wi-Fi is widely available in most cafes, restaurants, and hotels, but having everything ready on your phone will make for a seamless travel experience.

By following these travel tips and safety essentials, you'll be well-equipped to navigate Zadar with ease, ensuring that your trip is as enjoyable and stress-free as possible.

Whether you're exploring the historic Old Town, lounging on a beach, or venturing out on day trips, being prepared for the unexpected will only enhance your experience. Zadar is a welcoming and beautiful destination, and by taking simple steps to stay safe and informed, you'll be able to fully immerse yourself in everything this amazing city has to offer.

Happy travels, and remember: Zadar is a place where the unexpected often leads to the most unforgettable experiences.

Chapter 16: Money, Budgeting & Costs

When planning your trip to Zadar, one of the most crucial aspects of your journey will be understanding how to manage your money, keep an eye on your budget, and make the most of what this stunning Croatian city has to offer. Whether you're a backpacker trying to stretch your euros or a luxury traveler looking for indulgence without breaking the bank, Zadar can accommodate all kinds of budgets. In this chapter, I'll walk you through everything you need to know about money, budgeting, and costs, so you can focus on enjoying your adventure without worrying about your wallet.

16.1 Currency, ATMs, and Credit Cards

Croatia's official currency is the kuna (HRK), which may seem unfamiliar to many visitors, especially those coming from euro-using countries. While Croatia is part of the European Union, it has not yet adopted the euro, making the kuna essential for your travels. The exchange rate fluctuates, but you'll often find that 1 EUR equals around 7.5 HRK, although this may vary slightly depending on the season.

ATMs & Cash Withdrawals

ATMs are widely available throughout Zadar, especially in the Old Town, near the bus station, and in shopping centers. Most major banks, such as Zagrebačka Banka and Privredna Banka, have ATMs that allow you to withdraw kuna easily. However, keep in mind that ATM fees can vary, so it's a good idea to check with your home bank regarding any charges for international withdrawals.

Tip: When withdrawing cash, try to do so in larger amounts to avoid frequent fees. Additionally, avoid withdrawing small sums in places like touristy markets, where you might get charged higher fees.

Currency Exchange

While you can exchange money at various currency exchange offices or banks, the rates may not always be the best. Exchange rates in Zadar's tourist areas can be less favorable than those offered at a local bank or official exchange offices, so it's worth shopping around if you need to change cash.

If you're coming from the EU, you might also find that using a Euro-to-Kuna card at a local bank is one of the most convenient ways to exchange money without incurring hefty fees.

Credit & Debit Cards

Credit and debit cards are widely accepted in most establishments in Zadar, including restaurants, cafes, shops, and even some smaller attractions. Major cards such as Visa, Mastercard, and American Express are commonly used, but it's always wise to double-check with smaller vendors or accommodations before making purchases. However, don't assume that every place will accept cards, especially in more remote or traditional spots. It's a good idea to carry at least a small amount of cash for such occasions.

Tip: If you're planning on relying on your credit or debit card, be sure to notify your bank about your travel dates to avoid any problems with card transactions due to fraud protection. You wouldn't want to be stuck without access to funds while in a foreign country.

16.2 Typical Daily Costs & Budget Tips

Zadar is a fairly affordable destination, especially compared to larger European cities like Venice or Dubrovnik. However, like any place, the costs can add up depending on your travel style. Below, I've broken down a typical day's expenses so you can plan accordingly.

Accommodation Costs

Accommodation in Zadar can vary widely, depending on your preferences. You can find budget hostels or guesthouses starting at around 200 HRK per night for a basic room. If you're looking for mid-range hotels or private apartments, you can expect to pay between 400 HRK and 800 HRK per night. On the high end, luxury hotels, such as those near the marina or on the beach, will range from 1000 HRK upwards.

Tip: Booking in advance, especially during the summer months, is essential if you want to secure the best deals and avoid inflated prices. Look for accommodations in the Old Town for a more immersive experience, or check out options on the Zadar Peninsula for proximity to the beach.

Dining Out

Zadar offers a delightful mix of traditional Croatian food and Mediterranean-inspired cuisine. A typical meal at a casual restaurant can cost you anywhere from 70 HRK to 150 HRK per person, including a drink. If you're craving seafood, which Zadar is known for, expect to pay around 120 HRK for a hearty plate of fish or seafood pasta. At higher-end restaurants, expect to pay between 200 HRK to 500 HRK for a more refined dining experience, including wine.

For breakfast, a coffee and pastry at a local café can be as low as 20 HRK, making it an easy way to start your day without breaking the bank. If you're on a tight budget, opt for street food like a burek (a savory pastry) or ćevapi (grilled minced meat) from local vendors for around 25-50 HRK.

Tip: For a truly affordable meal, visit the Zadar City Market where you can find fresh produce, local cheeses, olives, and meats. Pick up some snacks for a picnic or grab an affordable lunch at one of the nearby bakeries.

Transportation

Zadar's public transport system is inexpensive and relatively easy to use. A single bus ticket within the city costs around 10 HRK, while tickets for longer journeys to nearby areas like Nin or Zadar's suburbs may range between 20 HRK and 40 HRK. Taxis are also available but can be more expensive, particularly if you're traveling a longer distance.

Tip: If you plan on taking public transport frequently, consider purchasing a multi-day pass to save money. Alternatively, walking is a great way to explore Zadar's compact city center.

16.3 How to Save While Traveling in Zadar

Traveling on a budget in Zadar is certainly possible, especially if you plan ahead and make some savvy choices. Below are my top tips for getting the most out of your Croatian adventure without overspending.

Use Free Attractions

Zadar is brimming with free or low-cost attractions that are well worth your time. The Sea Organ and Sun Salutation, two of Zadar's most famous landmarks, are completely free to visit. Enjoy the music of the sea or witness the breathtaking sunset from these iconic spots without spending a dime. Stroll through the Old Town and explore historical sites like St. Donatus Church, the Roman Forum, and the City Walls, all of which offer a rich cultural experience without costing anything.

Take Advantage of Local Markets

Instead of dining out at expensive restaurants every night, head to the Zadar City Market to buy fresh, local ingredients. You can find a wide range of fresh produce, meats, cheeses, and seafood, which makes for a delicious and affordable picnic on the beach or a home-cooked meal in your accommodation's kitchen. This is especially a great option if you're staying in an apartment or Airbnb with kitchen facilities.

Visit Off-Season

To experience Zadar at its most affordable, consider visiting during the shoulder seasons, late spring (May-June) or early autumn (September-October). During these months, accommodation rates are lower, the crowds are thinner, and the weather is still delightful. You'll also find that some attractions and tours offer discounted rates during this time.

Tip: Look for deals on accommodation and tours before your trip. Websites like Booking.com and Airbnb often offer great discounts for early bookings, especially in off-peak seasons.

Zadar offers a range of experiences for every kind of traveler, and with a little bit of planning, you can enjoy everything this stunning city has to offer without breaking the bank. From its affordable accommodation options to its fantastic dining and free cultural experiences, Zadar is a city that allows you to stretch your kuna while still having an unforgettable adventure. Remember to budget wisely, plan for the season, and be sure to enjoy the simple pleasures, Zadar is a place where experiences matter more than spending.

Chapter 17: Luxury Travel in Zadar

Zadar, with its charming old-world beauty and crystal-clear Adriatic waters, offers a luxurious escape for those seeking opulence and tranquility. While the city is known for its laid-back atmosphere, it's also home to a host of high-end experiences that cater to travelers who want the best of both worlds. Whether you're looking for a lavish hotel with panoramic sea views, a private yacht tour around the Kornati Islands, or a Michelin-starred meal under the stars, Zadar has something to indulge every sense. In this chapter, I'll take you through the finest offerings of luxury travel in Zadar, ensuring you experience the city's most exclusive and indulgent side.

17.1 Upscale Hotels & Private Villas

Zadar's luxury accommodations offer a combination of modern elegance and historical charm, giving guests the ultimate comfort and a true sense of place. If you're looking for an unforgettable stay, you'll be delighted by the high-end options available.

Falkensteiner Hotel & Spa Iadera

For a luxurious hotel experience, the Falkensteiner Hotel & Spa Iadera is hard to beat. Perched on the Punta Skala Peninsula, this five-star resort boasts spectacular views of the Adriatic Sea.

The hotel is designed with contemporary flair, featuring spacious rooms and suites with private terraces, sleek marble bathrooms, and floor-to-ceiling windows. But it's the hotel's spa that truly sets it apart. Acquapura Spa offers a range of indulgent treatments, from rejuvenating massages to detoxifying body wraps, ensuring that you leave feeling pampered and refreshed.

Almayer Art & Heritage Hotel

If you're seeking a more intimate and artistic atmosphere, Almayer Art & Heritage Hotel offers a unique blend of modern comfort and historical charm. Located within Zadar's Old Town, the boutique hotel is housed in a beautifully restored building that dates back to the 18th century.

Each room is tastefully decorated with artwork and furniture that reflect the city's rich history, while still offering all the modern luxuries you'd expect from a high-end hotel. The personalized service and exclusive atmosphere make it perfect for those who want to experience the elegance of the city's heritage while enjoying modern amenities.

Private Villas and Luxury Apartments

For a more secluded and personalized stay, consider booking a private villa or luxury apartment. Zadar's coastline is dotted with stunning properties that offer the ultimate privacy and comfort.

Think infinity pools overlooking the azure sea, spacious living areas, and personal chefs or butlers at your service. If you prefer something closer to nature, villas in the nearby countryside offer the perfect escape, with sprawling gardens and breathtaking views of the surrounding mountains. Booking a private villa allows you to experience Zadar at your own pace, without the constraints of hotel schedules or shared spaces.

17.2 Gourmet Dining & Private Chefs

Zadar is home to a vibrant culinary scene, with flavors influenced by its rich history and proximity to the sea. If you're a food connoisseur, you'll find plenty of opportunities for indulgence, from exquisite fine dining restaurants to private chefs crafting personalized meals.

Restaurant 2

If you're seeking a world-class dining experience, Restaurant 2 should be at the top of your list. Located in the heart of Zadar, this Michelin-starred restaurant blends traditional Croatian ingredients with innovative techniques. The tasting menu changes seasonally, showcasing the freshest produce from local farms and the Adriatic's abundant seafood. Each dish is a work of art, beautifully presented with an emphasis on flavor and texture.

Pair your meal with wines from a curated selection of Croatian vineyards, and you'll find yourself transported into a world of gastronomic delight.

The Sea Organ and the Sunset

For a truly unforgettable dining experience, consider enjoying a private meal at one of Zadar's top-notch restaurants while watching the sun set over the sea. Many high-end restaurants offer outdoor seating with panoramic views, creating the perfect backdrop for an evening of gourmet dining. The Sea Organ nearby provides a natural symphony as the waves crash against the pipes, adding an atmospheric touch to your evening.

Private Chef Experience

For those who want to enjoy a more intimate dining experience, hiring a private chef to prepare a meal in your villa or private apartment is a must. Several luxury concierge services in Zadar offer this option, with chefs crafting bespoke menus based on your tastes. Whether you want a multi-course tasting menu, a traditional Dalmatian feast, or a wine-pairing dinner, your private chef will ensure the experience is nothing short of extraordinary. Paired with a handpicked selection of local wines and ingredients, it's a dining experience you won't soon forget.

17.3 Bespoke Tours & Yacht Charters

The best way to explore Zadar's stunning coast and surrounding islands in style is with a bespoke tour or yacht charter. With its crystal-clear waters, hidden coves, and picturesque islands, the Zadar archipelago is a perfect playground for the discerning traveler.

Private Yacht Charter

Chartering a private yacht is one of the most luxurious ways to experience Zadar's coastline. With a dedicated crew to cater to your every need, you can explore the nearby Kornati National Park, often referred to as the "nautical paradise" of Croatia, or venture further out to the islands of Dugi Otok and Ugljan.

Spend your day swimming in secluded bays, snorkeling in untouched waters, or simply lounging on deck with a glass of local wine in hand. Some yachts come with additional amenities like a Jacuzzi, a fully stocked bar, and personalized itineraries that allow you to create your own dream day on the water.

Bespoke Cultural and Adventure Tours

If you prefer to stay on land, Zadar offers a variety of bespoke tours that can be tailored to your interests. For example, you can hire a private guide to take you through the Zadar Old Town, visiting the Roman Forum, the Church of St. Donatus, and other historical landmarks.

If you're an art lover, a personalized art tour can lead you through the city's galleries and museums, where you'll explore Zadar's unique blend of modern and ancient art. For nature lovers, bespoke hiking or cycling tours through the surrounding countryside are a great way to explore the natural beauty of the region, with a guide to ensure you don't miss any hidden gems.

17.4 High-End Wellness & Spa Experiences

After a day of indulgence, you'll want to relax and rejuvenate, and Zadar's wellness scene offers some of the finest spa experiences in the region. From serene spa resorts to exclusive wellness centers, you'll find plenty of opportunities to unwind.

Acquapura Spa at Falkensteiner Hotel & Spa Iadera

For a top-tier spa experience, the Acquapura Spa at Falkensteiner Hotel is one of the best in the area. With panoramic views of the Adriatic Sea, this spa offers an array of treatments designed to relax and revitalize. From massages and facials to thalassotherapy and beauty rituals, every treatment is tailored to your needs. You can also enjoy the hotel's wellness facilities, including the Finnish sauna, steam bath, and indoor pool.

Private Wellness Treatments

For a truly exclusive experience, consider booking a private wellness treatment in your villa or yacht. Several luxury concierge services in Zadar offer personalized wellness packages, which can include anything from yoga sessions with a private instructor to deep tissue massages and aromatherapy treatments. You can also request in-villa spa services, which are perfect for unwinding after a long day of exploration.

Zadar is a city that beautifully blends its rich history with modern luxury, offering travelers a wide array of indulgent experiences. Whether you're staying in an upscale hotel, enjoying a private yacht charter, savoring gourmet meals, or relaxing at a luxurious spa, the city provides the perfect backdrop for a lavish escape. The stunning Adriatic coast, with its serene waters and picturesque islands, combined with Zadar's sophisticated offerings, ensures that your luxury getaway will be nothing short of extraordinary.

Chapter 18: Guide for Solo Travelers

Zadar, with its perfect mix of history, nature, and welcoming local vibe, is an ideal destination for solo travelers. The beauty of this ancient city lies not just in its stunning sights but in its ability to offer peace and reflection, as well as the chance for adventure and connection. Whether you're seeking solitude by the sea, an immersive cultural experience, or the opportunity to meet like-minded travelers, Zadar is the place to be. Let me take you through why this gem of Croatia is perfect for solo adventures and how to make the most of your time here.

18.1 Why Zadar is Perfect for Solo Adventures

The first thing you'll notice about Zadar is its accessibility. The city feels compact, manageable, and easy to navigate, making it a great place to explore on your own. Unlike some bustling tourist hotspots, Zadar maintains a relaxed pace. You won't be rushing from one major sight to the next, and you certainly won't feel lost in a sea of tourists. Here, you can truly immerse yourself in the beauty and culture of the place, taking the time to explore at your own rhythm.

A City Steeped in History and Charm

Zadar is a historical treasure trove, offering you a rich, layered experience as you wander its ancient streets. The Roman Forum, with its crumbling pillars, feels like a time capsule from a bygone era, while the St. Donatus Church and Zadar Cathedral provide an intimate connection to the city's spiritual and architectural past.

What makes Zadar truly special, though, is the way it marries these historical landmarks with natural beauty. You can wander from the stone streets of the Old Town to the serene, blue expanse of the sea in a matter of minutes, giving you both the energy of a bustling city and the calm of the coast.

Secluded Spots for Reflection

For those moments when you want to escape the crowds and recharge, Zadar offers plenty of quiet corners. The Sea Organ, a marvel of modern design, is an excellent place to contemplate life. As the waves crash against the pipes, a soothing symphony emerges, perfect for solo reflection.

Or, take a walk to the Zadar City Walls and enjoy the panoramic views of the Adriatic and surrounding islands. These tranquil settings invite you to pause, breathe, and simply enjoy the moment. Zadar's natural beauty becomes an extension of your journey inward, offering time for introspection in a way few places do.

Easy to Explore on Foot

Zadar is incredibly walkable. You won't need to rely on complicated public transportation or taxis, which means you can spontaneously change course and follow whatever catches your interest. Want to wander into a quiet café or explore a local artisan shop? Zadar's Old Town and surrounding areas are designed for leisurely exploration, and as a solo traveler, you'll appreciate the freedom to follow your instincts without feeling rushed.

18.2 Meeting People & Social Travel

Although Zadar is a peaceful haven, it's not lacking in opportunities to meet fellow travelers. The small city atmosphere makes it easy to strike up conversations, whether you're in a cozy café or walking along the coastline. One of the joys of traveling solo here is the chance to mingle with locals and fellow explorers.

Solo-Friendly Social Activities

One of the best ways to meet people is by joining group activities. Walking tours are a great option to get to know the city better while meeting others. The guides here are friendly and often have interesting insights into the city's history, making it easy to bond over shared experiences.

In the evening, the city's relaxed café culture encourages mingling, especially around the People's Square or near the waterfront. Don't be shy to chat with the locals; the people of Zadar are known for their warmth and openness. The conversations often lead to hidden gems or local tips that you wouldn't find in a guidebook.

Cultural Events & Festivals

Zadar is also a hub for cultural events, and depending on when you visit, you'll have a chance to experience some truly unique activities. During the summer months, the Zadar Summer Festival fills the city with music, theater, and performances, offering a perfect environment for meeting people with similar interests.

In addition, the Zadar Film Festival and local art exhibitions provide great opportunities for both cultural immersion and social interaction. Even in the off-season, there are smaller local events and gatherings, making it easy to find like-minded travelers and locals to share experiences with.

Cafés and Restaurants for Solo Dining

Zadar's cafés are perfect for solo dining, as they offer an inviting atmosphere to enjoy a meal and people-watch. I recommend heading to Bistro Gourmet Kalelarga, where you can indulge in Mediterranean-inspired dishes while soaking in the vibrant energy of the city.

Many of the cafés in the Old Town have outdoor seating, allowing you to relax, sip a coffee, and observe the flow of daily life. Solo dining doesn't have to be lonely, it can be a chance to immerse yourself in local culture, savor authentic Croatian cuisine, and perhaps strike up a conversation with someone at the next table.

18.3 Safety & Comfort Tips

Zadar is one of the safest cities you can visit in Europe, making it ideal for solo travelers. That said, there are always practical steps you can take to ensure your trip is as smooth and comfortable as possible. Here are my top safety and comfort tips:

Staying Safe in Zadar

Zadar is a city that thrives on peace and hospitality, but like any destination, it's important to stay aware. Petty crime, such as pickpocketing, can occasionally occur in crowded areas, so always keep your belongings close, especially in tourist hotspots.

When you're wandering the narrow alleyways or the lively Narodni trg (People's Square), keep your wallet in a secure pocket or a crossbody bag. If you're heading out in the evening, especially to more secluded areas like Kolovare Beach, use a little extra caution, but rest assured that Zadar is generally very safe.

Transportation & Getting Around

Getting around Zadar is simple and convenient. Most of the city's main attractions are within walking distance, so you'll rarely need to take a taxi. However, if you want to explore beyond the Old Town, public buses are readily available and affordable. For those looking to venture further afield, Zadar is well connected to other Croatian cities via buses and ferries.

Solo travelers often appreciate the ease with which you can move around Zadar's surrounding areas, whether it's hopping on a ferry to Ugljan Island or catching a bus to the Kornati National Park for a day trip.

Comfortable Solo Stays

Finding the right place to stay is crucial for solo travelers. Zadar offers a range of accommodation options that cater to different needs. Hostels like The Hostel Zadar are perfect for meeting other young travelers, while boutique hotels like Almayer Art & Heritage Hotel offer a more private and peaceful atmosphere.

If you want to feel completely at home, consider renting an apartment, where you can enjoy a more private experience while still being close to everything the city has to offer.

Zadar is the kind of place that invites solo travelers to slow down and truly absorb the beauty of the world around them. Whether you're enjoying a moment of tranquility by the Sea Organ, exploring ancient Roman ruins, or meeting fellow travelers at a local café, there's something incredibly rewarding about exploring Zadar on your own. The city offers a perfect mix of cultural experiences, social opportunities, and personal reflection, everything a solo traveler could want. So, pack your bag, put on your walking shoes, and get ready to explore this beautiful city at your own pace.

Chapter 19: Traveling with Family & Kids

Traveling with family in tow often requires a little more planning, but the rewards are immense, and Zadar is the perfect destination for creating memorable experiences with loved ones. With its fascinating mix of history, nature, and a laid-back atmosphere, the city offers a variety of activities that will keep both kids and adults entertained. Whether you're exploring ancient ruins or swimming in the crystal-clear Adriatic, Zadar has something for every family member. Let me guide you through this beautiful city and share some insights that will help you have a fun, stress-free vacation with your little ones.

19.1 Kid-Friendly Activities & Attractions

Zadar may be known for its historical sights, but there's no shortage of exciting, kid-friendly activities to enjoy here. The city's welcoming atmosphere and abundance of outdoor spaces make it an ideal spot for families looking to enjoy a mix of adventure and relaxation.

1. The Sea Organ and Greeting to the Sun

One of the highlights of Zadar for children is the Sea Organ, an architectural marvel that combines art with nature. Located right by the water, this installation uses the movement of the waves to create music as it passes through pipes built into the promenade. Children will be mesmerized by the sound and the chance to play their own tunes simply by interacting with the sea. It's not only fun for kids but also a great spot for parents to relax while soaking in the Adriatic breeze.

Next door is the Greeting to the Sun, a stunning light installation that dazzles at night. The solar-powered discs light up in vibrant colors, offering a visual spectacle that's perfect for children and adults alike. This combination of sound and light is an unforgettable experience for families, especially in the early evening when the sunsets over the sea are nothing short of magical.

2. Zadar's Beaches

Zadar's beaches are another big draw for families. Kolovare Beach, located near the city center, is perfect for younger children, with shallow, warm waters that make it easy for little ones to splash around. There are plenty of beachside cafés, where you can take a break from the sun while keeping an eye on the kids.

If you're looking for more space to spread out, head to Borik Beach or Punta Bajlo, which are less crowded and ideal for family-friendly swimming and sandcastle building.

3. The Zadar Archaeological Museum & Roman Forum

For families with older children who are interested in history, the Zadar Archaeological Museum offers fascinating exhibits that will spark their curiosity. Located in a historic building, it provides insights into Zadar's rich past, from its Roman and medieval roots to its more recent history.

Nearby, the Roman Forum invites you to wander through ancient ruins, where kids can explore and imagine what life was like centuries ago. The open-air setting gives the perfect balance of education and adventure, offering space for kids to roam freely while learning about the past.

4. Fun Park Biograd

Just a short drive from Zadar, Fun Park Biograd is the perfect day trip for families looking for more excitement. This amusement park is packed with rides, water attractions, and fun for all ages. From roller coasters and bumper cars to water slides and splash zones, it's a great place to let loose and have some family fun. It's the perfect way to take a break from sightseeing and give the kids a chance to enjoy a day of pure fun.

19.2 Family-Friendly Restaurants & Hotels

When you're traveling with family, finding the right places to eat and stay is key. Zadar offers a fantastic selection of family-friendly restaurants and hotels that cater to all your needs while providing a welcoming atmosphere for your little ones.

1.   Family-Friendly   Dining   in   Zadar
Zadar's restaurant scene is diverse, and there are plenty of options for families. Pet Bunara is a wonderful choice for families seeking local cuisine in a cozy setting. The restaurant offers a range of traditional Croatian dishes, and the staff is incredibly accommodating, making it easy for families to enjoy a relaxed meal together. For a more casual experience, head to 4 Kantuna, a laid-back eatery offering fresh seafood and hearty local fare. The outdoor seating area is perfect for families to sit, eat, and enjoy the sea breeze.

If you're craving pizza, Konoba Skoblar offers an excellent selection of pies that kids will love, and it's located near the beach, so you can enjoy your meal while overlooking the sea. For those times when the kids are craving something quick and easy, the many cafés and snack bars along the Riva Promenade offer everything from sandwiches to ice cream.

2. Family-Friendly Accommodation in Zadar

Zadar is home to a range of family-friendly hotels and accommodations that combine comfort, convenience, and a welcoming atmosphere. Falkensteiner Hotel & Spa in Borik is a great option for families looking for a luxurious experience. With spacious rooms, a family-friendly pool, and easy access to the beach, it's a place where both parents and kids can relax and enjoy. The hotel also offers a kids' club and activities that will keep the little ones entertained while the adults take some time to unwind.

For those seeking a more homely experience, renting an apartment can be a great choice. There are plenty of family-oriented rentals in the Old Town and near the beaches, providing flexibility, space, and a chance to live like a local. With a kitchen at your disposal, you can cook meals together as a family and explore the city on your own schedule.

19.3 Tips for Stress-Free Family Travel

Traveling with kids can be challenging at times, but with a little preparation, Zadar offers a seamless and enjoyable family experience. Here are a few tips to make your trip more relaxed and stress-free:

1. Pack Smart

When traveling with kids, make sure to pack essentials like snacks, water, sunscreen, and baby wipes. You'll find that Zadar has everything you need, but having a few familiar items on hand can make a big difference. Also, don't forget lightweight strollers or carriers for younger children, as Zadar's cobblestone streets can sometimes be tricky for traditional strollers.

2. Plan for Downtime

While Zadar offers plenty to do, it's important to build in some downtime. Take a break from sightseeing and spend time enjoying the beach, relaxing in a café, or exploring the parks. This gives everyone a chance to recharge and ensures that the trip doesn't feel overwhelming for anyone.

3. Stay Flexible

Kids often have a different pace when it comes to sightseeing, so be flexible with your itinerary. Allow for spontaneous stops, whether it's grabbing a gelato on the Riva or playing in a park. Zadar's relaxed atmosphere makes it easy to go with the flow and adjust your plans as needed.

4. Travel in Off-Peak Seasons

If possible, consider visiting Zadar in the shoulder seasons, early spring or late autumn. The weather is still lovely, but the crowds are thinner, which makes it easier to enjoy the attractions without the stress of long lines or busy restaurants.

Zadar is an excellent destination for family travel, offering a mix of historical charm, natural beauty, and plenty of activities for kids of all ages. From playing by the Sea Organ to enjoying the stunning beaches, there's no shortage of fun, family-friendly attractions. With its welcoming atmosphere, variety of dining and accommodation options, and abundance of kid-friendly activities, Zadar provides an ideal backdrop for making lasting memories with your loved ones. Pack your bags, gather your family, and get ready for an unforgettable adventure in one of Croatia's most enchanting cities.

Chapter 20: Sustainable & Responsible Travel

Traveling responsibly and sustainably isn't just about reducing your carbon footprint or minimizing waste, it's about creating meaningful connections with the places you visit and leaving them better than you found them. Zadar, with its rich history, beautiful nature, and vibrant community, is the perfect destination for responsible travel. The city's dedication to preserving its heritage, culture, and environment is evident in its numerous sustainable initiatives, and as a traveler, you can help by making thoughtful choices that contribute to the well-being of both the local community and the planet. In this chapter, I'll share practical tips and recommendations on how to enjoy Zadar while traveling in an eco-friendly and responsible way.

20.1 Eco-Friendly Tours & Operators

When it comes to exploring Zadar, one of the best ways to stay connected to the local environment is by choosing eco-friendly tours and activities. Zadar offers a variety of sustainable travel options that allow you to explore its natural beauty without harming it.

1. Exploring Nature with Eco-Tours

If you're a nature enthusiast, there are several eco-friendly tours available that showcase the stunning landscapes of Zadar. The Krka National Park and Paklenica National Park are must-visit destinations, and many tour operators offer small-group or private tours that use environmentally conscious practices. These tours often include a local guide who can share the park's natural history and emphasize the importance of conservation. You'll get to hike through lush forests, admire waterfalls, and enjoy the pristine surroundings, all while learning about the sustainable efforts in place to protect these precious ecosystems.

For a more adventurous experience, consider a kayaking tour along the Zadar coastline. Several eco-conscious operators offer kayaking experiences where you can paddle through the serene waters of the Adriatic, exploring hidden coves and small islands. These tours are not only great for the environment, as they avoid emissions from motorized boats, but they also give you an intimate view of the coastline, away from the crowds.

2. Eco-Friendly Boat Tours

Zadar's stunning archipelago is another highlight, and taking a boat tour is one of the best ways to experience the islands. Opt for an eco-friendly boat that runs on solar power or electric engines, reducing the environmental impact of your excursion.

These tours often focus on sustainability, educating visitors on the importance of marine conservation. As you cruise around the islands, you might spot sea turtles, dolphins, and other marine life, making this an ideal way to support wildlife conservation efforts.

3. Bike and Walking Tours

Zadar's compact Old Town is perfect for exploring on foot, and there are several walking tours available that focus on the city's history and architecture. Many of these tours emphasize sustainable travel by keeping the group sizes small and walking at a leisurely pace to minimize environmental impact.

For those who want to cover more ground while still staying eco-friendly, bike tours are a great option. Zadar has been investing in bike-friendly infrastructure, and biking around the city allows you to experience it from a different perspective while reducing your carbon footprint.

20.2 Supporting Local Artisans & Businesses

Sustainable travel goes beyond minimizing waste, it's also about supporting the local community and economy. One of the best ways to do this in Zadar is by shopping at local markets, dining at family-run restaurants, and purchasing handmade goods from artisans.

1. Visiting Local Markets

Zadar's City Market (Tržnica Zadar) is a vibrant and authentic place where you can buy fresh, locally grown produce, handmade goods, and artisanal products. The market is a great place to interact with local vendors, learn about the produce that's in season, and get a sense of the flavors that define the region. Shopping at local markets not only supports small-scale farmers and producers but also helps preserve traditional agricultural practices that are vital to the local economy.

For an even more personal experience, consider visiting local craft shops that sell handmade jewelry, textiles, and ceramics. Many artisans in Zadar focus on sustainable materials and eco-friendly production methods, so when you buy a piece, you're not only getting a beautiful souvenir but also contributing to the preservation of traditional Croatian crafts.

2. Dining with a Focus on Sustainability

Zadar is home to many restaurants that pride themselves on serving locally sourced, organic, and sustainable food. One standout is Restaurant 4 Kantuna, where the chef focuses on using ingredients sourced from nearby farms and fishermen. The restaurant also works to minimize food waste by using every part of the ingredients, and the menu changes with the seasons to ensure the freshest produce is served.

Another fantastic option is Konoba Skoblar, a family-run restaurant where traditional Dalmatian dishes are made using locally sourced meats and seafood, supporting small fishermen and farmers in the region.

As a responsible traveler, choose dining establishments that embrace farm-to-table practices and avoid chains or mass-produced food. By supporting these local eateries, you help ensure that the economic benefits stay within the community and that sustainable practices are encouraged.

20.3 Travel with Less Waste

Reducing waste while traveling is not only beneficial for the environment, but it also helps you enjoy your trip in a more mindful and intentional way. Zadar is a city that is increasingly focused on sustainability, and as a traveler, you can easily contribute to this effort.

1. Bring Reusable Items

One of the simplest ways to reduce waste in Zadar is by bringing reusable items such as water bottles, shopping bags, and travel utensils. Zadar's climate can be hot in summer, and you'll likely be buying drinks throughout the day. Instead of relying on single-use plastic bottles, bring a reusable water bottle to refill at public water fountains, which are widely available.

Many cafés and restaurants also encourage guests to use reusable containers, so bring your own coffee cup or food container when picking up takeout.

Additionally, avoid using plastic bags when shopping at local markets or stores. Bring your own reusable bag for groceries or souvenirs, which helps reduce the plastic waste that often ends up in the sea.

2. Support Eco-Conscious Hotels and Accommodation

When choosing where to stay, consider booking accommodations that prioritize sustainability. Several hotels in Zadar are committed to reducing their environmental impact through energy-efficient practices, water conservation, and waste reduction. Hotel Bastion is an excellent example, offering eco-friendly amenities such as energy-saving lighting and recycling programs. If you're looking for a more personal experience, consider renting an apartment or staying in a local guesthouse that uses eco-friendly cleaning products and sustainable materials.

3. Mindful Transportation

Zadar has an excellent public transportation system, making it easy to get around the city without relying on taxis or rental cars. The bus network is well-connected and affordable, allowing you to explore the city and surrounding areas while reducing your carbon footprint.

For a more eco-conscious option, consider renting a bicycle or using an electric scooter, which are both popular and efficient modes of transportation in Zadar.

Sustainable travel is all about making thoughtful, responsible choices that contribute to the well-being of the environment and local communities. Zadar provides a wonderful opportunity to explore Croatia's natural beauty, rich culture, and vibrant community while practicing eco-friendly habits. Whether you're choosing eco-tours, supporting local businesses, or reducing your waste, every small action counts toward making a positive impact. So, as you plan your trip to this stunning city, remember that sustainable travel isn't just about what you leave behind, it's about creating meaningful connections and preserving the places you visit for future generations to enjoy.

Chapter 21: Capture the Moment: Photography & Social Media

Zadar is one of those rare places that seems designed for capturing moments of sheer beauty. Whether you're gazing at the sparkling blue of the Adriatic, wandering through narrow cobblestone streets steeped in history, or marveling at the breathtaking sunset, every corner of this city is a potential masterpiece. As a seasoned traveler with an eye for aesthetics, I've spent hours behind the lens, and in this chapter, I'll share the best photography spots in Zadar, along with tips on how to get the most out of your photos. And, of course, for those who want to show off their experience on social media, I've included a guide to the most Instagrammable and TikTok-worthy locations.

21.1 Best Photo Spots in Zadar

Zadar is a treasure trove of photogenic scenes. From ancient Roman ruins to modern art installations, the city offers an incredible range of subjects for your photography.

1. Zadar Old Town

The heart of Zadar, the Old Town, is an absolute must-see for any photographer. This historic district is an elegant blend of Roman, Venetian, and modern influences.

Narrow streets wind through ancient stone walls, with glimpses of red-tiled roofs peeking out between tall buildings. Narodni trg (People's Square) is a central gathering place that's perfect for capturing the charm of the Old Town, with the looming Church of St. Donatus in the background.

2. The Sea Organ and Greeting to the Sun

Two of Zadar's most iconic sights, the Sea Organ and the Greeting to the Sun, are located just off the Riva (seafront promenade). The Sea Organ, designed by architect Nikola Bašić, is an architectural marvel that combines art and nature. As the waves hit the steps, they create music, a captivating sight and sound that's impossible to resist photographing. Right next door is the Greeting to the Sun, a modern light installation that features solar panels arranged in a circular pattern. At sunset, it transforms into a dazzling display of light and color, offering the perfect backdrop for your photos.

3. Zadar's City Walls

The Roman Forum and the City Walls are essential photographic subjects. The Forum, dating back to the 1st century BC, is the perfect spot for capturing the essence of Zadar's ancient history. The surrounding city walls, especially near the Land Gate, offer stunning views of the town and the sea, and they're particularly magical during the golden hour when the soft light spills over the stone structures.

4. The Islands of Zadar Archipelago

A boat ride out to the nearby islands is another fantastic photographic opportunity. The islands, like Ugljan and Pasman, are known for their pristine nature and secluded beaches. If you're after a more natural setting, the islands offer rugged coastlines, untouched nature, and breathtaking views back toward Zadar.

21.2 Photography Tips: Light, Angles & Timing

Now that you know where to go, let's talk about how to capture the essence of Zadar in the best way possible. Photography is not just about the subject; it's about the way you interact with it. Here are some of my top tips for making your shots stand out.

1. Embrace the Golden Hour

The golden hour, the period just after sunrise or before sunset, is often hailed as the best time to photograph landscapes. Zadar is no exception. The soft, warm light creates long shadows and enhances the colors of the sky and buildings.

I recommend getting up early to catch the sunrise over the sea or strolling along the Riva in the late afternoon to catch the sun setting behind the islands. It's during this time that the Sea Organ also creates its most enchanting sounds, providing a perfect soundtrack to your photos.

2. Play with Reflections

Zadar's shimmering Adriatic waters offer countless opportunities for reflection shots. One of my favorite tricks is to take advantage of the reflections in the sea near the Greeting to the Sun. You can also get creative with the water reflections in the narrow alleys or small harbor areas, where the water mirrors the colorful boats and buildings around them.

3. Find Unique Angles

When photographing iconic sites like St. Donatus Church, don't just aim for the usual wide-angle shot. Experiment with angles. For example, shoot from a low angle to make the church seem even more imposing against the clear sky. Alternatively, capture the intricate stone details of the Roman Forum with close-ups or abstract shots that highlight the textures of the ruins.

4. Focus on Details

Zadar is rich in history, and there's beauty in the details. Look for small moments, like the delicate Roman columns peeking out of crumbling walls or the texture of Dalmatian stone on the ancient buildings. These details can help tell the story of the city in a more intimate and creative way. Even something as simple as a close-up of a coffee cup at one of Zadar's cafes can evoke a sense of place.

21.3 Instagram & TikTok-Worthy Places

For those of you looking to boost your Instagram feed or TikTok account, Zadar offers no shortage of visually striking spots that are perfect for social media. Here are some of the top places to get those scroll-stopping shots.

1. The Sea Organ at Sunset

Let's start with the obvious: the Sea Organ. The combination of natural sound and beautiful surroundings makes it the ultimate Instagrammable spot. At sunset, when the colors of the sky reflect on the water, this spot becomes almost otherworldly. Whether you're sitting on the steps, capturing the waves crashing over the organ, or snapping a photo of the Greeting to the Sun glowing in the background, it's guaranteed to impress your followers.

2. Zadar's Streets at Night

After the sun sets, Zadar takes on a completely different character. The streets of the Old Town are quiet and peaceful, and the soft lighting from the street lamps casts an ethereal glow on the stone buildings. This is the perfect time to get shots of the city's architecture at night. The Roman Forum looks particularly striking when illuminated, as does the Land Gate with its majestic stone arches.

3. The View from the Bell Tower of St. Anastasia's Cathedral

For a sweeping panoramic shot of the city, head to the top of the Bell Tower of St. Anastasia's Cathedral. The climb is worth it when you get to see the stunning vista of Zadar, with the blue sea stretching out into the distance and the jagged peaks of nearby islands dotting the horizon. The contrast of red rooftops against the deep blue sky makes for a striking photo.

4. Exploring the Islands

The islands off the coast of Zadar provide the perfect backdrop for stunning nature shots. Whether you're hiking up to a secluded viewpoint, lounging on a quiet beach, or kayaking through the turquoise waters, these islands are a hidden gem for travel photographers. For TikTokers, the crystal-clear waters and breathtaking landscapes are ideal for short, cinematic videos.

Zadar is an absolute photographer's paradise, offering everything from historic Roman ruins to natural wonders that seem straight out of a postcard. Whether you're an amateur photographer or a seasoned pro, there's no shortage of opportunities to capture the perfect shot. By playing with light, experimenting with angles, and visiting the city's most iconic spots, you'll come away with photos that are as timeless as Zadar itself.

And with Instagram and TikTok providing the perfect platform to share your journey, you'll be able to show your friends and followers exactly why Zadar deserves a place on every traveler's bucket list. Happy shooting!

Chapter 22: Avoiding Common Pitfalls

Traveling to a new destination is always an exciting adventure, but like all journeys, it comes with a few bumps along the way. Whether it's overhyped attractions, common mistakes, or misunderstandings of local customs, even the most seasoned travelers can fall into traps if they're not careful. In this chapter, I'll guide you through the pitfalls that many visitors to Zadar face and offer alternatives, tips, and local insights to help ensure your trip is smooth, enjoyable, and full of authentic experiences. Let's dive in and avoid the common pitfalls together.

22.1 Overrated Attractions & Alternatives

Zadar, like any popular destination, has its share of well-known spots that attract the crowds. While these places are certainly worth seeing, they can sometimes feel overrated, especially when the sheer volume of tourists detracts from their charm. But fear not, Zadar has plenty of hidden gems and alternative experiences that will allow you to enjoy the city at its best.

The   Sea   Organ   and   Greeting   to   the   Sun

Let's start with Zadar's most famous attraction: the Sea Organ and the Greeting to the Sun. Both are visually stunning and culturally significant, but if you visit during peak tourist hours, you may find them overcrowded, making it harder to enjoy the unique atmosphere. The Sea Organ, which creates beautiful music from the sea's waves, can be drowned out by the sound of chatter and camera shutters.

Alternative: Visit early in the morning or just before sunset to experience these iconic sites without the crowds. The soft morning light on the Sea Organ, combined with the quiet of the early hours, offers a much more peaceful, personal experience. And don't miss the Sunset over the Adriatic, this natural spectacle, visible from the Sea Organ, is equally enchanting when witnessed in solitude.

The Roman Forum

The Roman Forum is another must-see, but it's often filled with groups of tourists and their guides. While it's undeniably important for understanding Zadar's Roman heritage, its small size can feel cramped with so many people around.

Alternative: Head over to the Zadar Archaeological Museum nearby, where you'll find fascinating artifacts from the Roman period in a quieter, more intimate setting. You can also visit Kopnena Vrata, the Land Gate, for a panoramic view of the city and its walls, another great way to learn about Zadar's history without the crowds.

St. Donatus Church

This ancient church, one of Zadar's most iconic landmarks, can be beautiful, but it's often surrounded by tourists during the day.

Alternative: If you want a more peaceful, meditative experience, visit St. Mary's Church, which is less crowded and equally charming. The interior features an impressive collection of medieval art and a serene atmosphere perfect for reflection.

22.2 Mistakes Travelers Often Make

Even experienced travelers can make mistakes, especially when they're unfamiliar with the local customs, transportation, or environment. Here are a few common missteps that visitors to Zadar often make, and how to avoid them.

1.   Not   Respecting   Local   Dining   Hours
In many tourist destinations, meals are served at all hours of the day, but Zadar follows a more traditional schedule. Local restaurants often open for lunch from 12:00 PM to 3:00 PM and then reopen for dinner around 6:00 PM, lasting until 10:00 PM or later.

If you try to dine too early or too late, you might find many places closed or operating at reduced capacity.

Tip: Plan your meals around local dining hours, and consider enjoying a relaxing stroll along the Riva promenade in between meal times. Zadar's cafe culture is a wonderful way to experience the city's slower pace of life.

2. Overlooking the Local Islands

Many tourists get so caught up in the city itself that they forget about the beautiful islands surrounding Zadar. The islands of Ugljan, Pašman, and Dugi Otok are rich in natural beauty, offer quiet beaches, and are perfect for day trips.

Tip: Don't make the mistake of skipping the islands. Take a boat trip to Ugljan Island and enjoy its lush greenery and tranquil beaches. Or, for a bit of adventure, rent a kayak and explore the hidden coves of Dugi Otok.

3. Rushing Through the Old Town

Zadar's Old Town is filled with history, charm, and character. Too many visitors rush through the Old Town, trying to tick off every major landmark in one go, which often means they miss the small, beautiful details that make the city so special.

Tip: Take your time. Wander through the cobbled streets and discover hidden squares, local art galleries, and quiet cafes. Sit down in a local café for a coffee or glass of wine and soak in the atmosphere. Zadar isn't about ticking off a list of must-sees; it's about taking in the essence of the city at your own pace.

4.   Not   Understanding   Local   Etiquette

Croatians, especially in more traditional areas like Zadar, appreciate polite and respectful behavior. It's considered courteous to greet people with a friendly "Dobar dan" (Good day) when entering shops or restaurants. Also, when meeting someone for the first time, a firm handshake is the norm.

Tip: Brush up on a few basic Croatian phrases, and always be polite and respectful to the locals. They're incredibly warm and welcoming, but showing respect for their culture goes a long way in creating meaningful interactions.

22.3 What Locals Wish Tourists Knew

If you really want to experience Zadar like a local, it's helpful to know what the people who call this city home wish visitors understood about their culture, lifestyle, and the city itself. Here are a few insights that will enhance your trip.

1. Zadar Isn't Just for Tourists, It's a Living, Breathing City
Many tourists come to Zadar and think of it as merely a holiday destination. While it is undoubtedly one of the most beautiful places to visit, Zadar is also a vibrant city with a thriving local population. Tourists often overlook this aspect, focusing solely on the touristy parts of the city.

Tip: Spend time in neighborhoods outside the tourist hotspots. Visit local markets, walk through residential areas, and enjoy conversations with locals who are eager to share their city. Zadar is as much about its people as it is about its sights.

2. The Pace of Life is Slower Here
Croatia's Mediterranean lifestyle means that Zadar moves at a slower pace. This isn't a city built for fast-paced, high-energy tourism. It's about savoring the small moments, whether that's a slow meal by the sea or a relaxing sunset walk.

Tip: Embrace the slow pace. Take time to sit and enjoy a glass of wine at a seaside cafe, or linger on the steps of the Sea Organ, listening to the rhythmic sounds of the ocean. Don't rush your experience; let the city's rhythm become your own.

3. Don't Overlook Local Food and Drink
Zadar's food scene is far more than just pizza and pasta. The city's cuisine is rooted in Mediterranean traditions, with an emphasis on fresh seafood, locally grown produce, and delicious olive oil.

Too often, visitors fall for international chains or familiar tourist spots instead of exploring authentic, local eateries.

Tip: Seek out hidden gems, small family-run restaurants, and market stalls where you can sample traditional dishes like pašticada (a slow-cooked beef stew) or sardines on the grill. The Zadar Farmers' Market is a fantastic place to experience fresh, local ingredients, and if you're lucky, you might get a few tips from the vendors on how to cook Croatian specialties.

By avoiding the common pitfalls, you'll unlock the true magic of Zadar. Whether it's taking your time to explore the lesser-known attractions, respecting the local customs, or simply embracing the slow pace of life, Zadar offers an authentic experience that goes beyond the typical tourist trail. The city's charm lies not just in its historic landmarks but in the way it invites you to immerse yourself in its atmosphere, culture, and people. Keep these insights in mind, and you'll have a more fulfilling, enjoyable, and meaningful trip to one of Croatia's most beautiful destinations.

Chapter 23: Departure & Final Travel Tips

As your time in Zadar comes to an end, there's always that bittersweet feeling, a sense of wanting to stay just a little longer, yet eager to take home memories that will last a lifetime. Your departure doesn't have to be rushed or stressful. Instead, it can be the perfect moment to reflect on the experiences you've had, make the most of your last hours, and leave this beautiful city with a smile on your face. In this chapter, I'll walk you through some essential last-minute tips for your departure, including shopping, packing, and ensuring a smooth transition from Zadar to wherever you're heading next.

23.1 Last-Minute Shopping & Packing List

Before you bid farewell to Zadar, there are a few key items you'll want to pick up to remember your time in this enchanting city. Whether you're looking for unique souvenirs or practical travel essentials for the journey, Zadar has plenty of opportunities for last-minute shopping.

Shopping for Souvenirs

Zadar is known for its rich history and vibrant local culture, which is reflected in its many charming shops and markets. To bring home a piece of Zadar, head to Zadar's Central Market (Tržnica Zadar), where you can find fresh produce, handmade goods, and local specialties. It's the perfect place to pick up olive oil, homemade jams, or local honey, all of which are perfect for gifts or to enjoy back home.

For a more artisanal touch, head to the old town where you'll find boutiques selling handcrafted jewelry, local ceramics, and traditional textiles. Be sure to check out the small galleries tucked in the winding streets where you can find original artworks by local artists, capturing the essence of Zadar and its surroundings.

If you're looking for something unique, consider purchasing a bottle of Maraschino liqueur, a specialty of Zadar. It's made from the Marasca cherries grown in the region, and it's a wonderful way to bring the taste of the Dalmatian coast back with you.

Packing List for Your Return Journey

When packing for your return journey, it's important to think about the weather conditions you might encounter in the coming days. Zadar, with its Mediterranean climate, is typically sunny and warm, but depending on the time of year, you may need to pack accordingly.

- **Essentials**: Don't forget your charger, camera, and any documents like tickets or itineraries. Zadar's old town streets are picturesque, so make sure your camera is fully charged to capture any last-minute moments.

- **Comfortable Footwear**: If you've been walking around Zadar, you've probably noticed how uneven some of the ancient streets can be. A sturdy pair of walking shoes will make your last day of exploration much more comfortable.

- **Sunscreen and Sunglasses**: Zadar's sunny weather can be deceivingly intense, especially in the summer months. Don't forget to reapply sunscreen throughout the day.

- **Light Layer**: If you're visiting in the evening, temperatures can dip a bit, so a light jacket or sweater might be useful for those sunset strolls along the sea.

23.2 Airport Transfers & Leaving Zadar Smoothly

Now that you've picked up your souvenirs and packed your bags, the next step is ensuring that you can get to the airport smoothly, leaving Zadar without any stress. Whether you're flying back home or to your next destination, here are some tips to make the journey to the airport as seamless as possible.

Getting to Zadar Airport (ZAD)

Zadar's small yet efficient airport, Zadar International Airport (ZAD), is located around 12 kilometers outside the city center, making it easily accessible. You have several options for getting there:

- **Taxi**: Taxis are available throughout the city, and the ride to the airport will take about 20 minutes. Be sure to confirm the fare before you get in, as rates may vary. A taxi ride typically costs around 150-200 HRK (Croatian kuna).

- **Airport Shuttle**: If you're traveling with a group or looking for a more economical option, the airport shuttle bus runs regularly from the city center to the airport, with tickets priced at around 30 HRK. This is a good option if you're on a budget or don't mind a few extra minutes of travel.

- **Private Transfers**: If you prefer a more luxurious experience, you can book a private transfer in advance. Many hotels also offer shuttle services for their guests, so be sure to check with your accommodation if this is an option.

Regardless of the mode of transport, make sure to leave with plenty of time to spare. The airport, while small, can get busy during peak seasons, and you'll want to have enough time to navigate through check-in and security.

Travel Tips for Smooth Departures

- **Arrive Early**: I always recommend arriving at least two hours before your flight departs, especially if you're traveling internationally. While Zadar's airport is small, the lines can get long during busy seasons.

- **Currency and Payment**: Most shops and services at the airport accept credit cards, but it's a good idea to exchange any remaining kuna back into your home currency if you have any leftover.

- **Baggage**: If you've purchased anything delicate, like pottery or glass, make sure it's securely packed. Zadar's airport has limited baggage assistance, so packing fragile items carefully is key to ensuring they make it home in one piece.

23.3 Making Your Last Day Memorable

While it's tempting to rush to the airport to catch your flight, I always find that the last day in any city offers the perfect opportunity to savor a few more experiences before you leave. In Zadar, there are several ways to make your last day one to remember, without feeling the pressure to cram in too many activities.

Stroll Through the Old Town

Before you leave, take a final stroll through Zadar's Old Town. The quiet streets early in the morning are a beautiful contrast to the hustle and bustle of midday, and they offer the perfect chance to reflect on your time in the city. Stop by your favorite café for a coffee or a pastry, and take in the sights you've fallen in love with over the past days.

Catch One Last Sunset

Zadar is famous for its stunning sunsets, so what better way to say goodbye than with one final view of the sun sinking into the Adriatic Sea? Head to the Riva or the Sea Organ to enjoy the sunset, or take a boat ride around the nearby islands to experience this magical moment from the water. If you've had the chance to take a sunset cruise, it's one of the most unforgettable ways to see Zadar for the last time.

Enjoy a Final Meal

Don't rush your final meal. Take your time at one of Zadar's local restaurants, and savor the flavors of the Dalmatian coast one last time. Order the grilled fish, black risotto, or pašticada, whatever dish you've enjoyed most during your stay. Pair it with a glass of local wine or rakija to toast to your time in Zadar.

As you prepare for your departure, take a moment to reflect on the unforgettable memories you've made in Zadar. Whether it's the mesmerizing sunsets, the ancient Roman ruins, or the serene sound of the Sea Organ, the city has likely left a lasting impression on you. By following these tips for your final day, shopping for unique souvenirs, ensuring a smooth airport transfer, and savoring every moment, you can end your trip on the highest note. Safe travels, and may your memories of Zadar continue to inspire your next adventure.

Chapter 24: Appendix & Resources

As your adventure in Zadar draws to a close, having a solid collection of resources and practical information can be the key to making your trip smooth and stress-free. From knowing whom to call in case of an emergency to learning a few essential Croatian phrases, this appendix will equip you with the tools needed to navigate Zadar and Croatia with ease. Here, I've compiled the most important travel information, helpful tips, and resources that will serve you throughout your stay.

24.1 Emergency Numbers & Tourist Help Lines

Whether you're exploring the historic ruins of Zadar or taking a dip in the Adriatic, it's always a good idea to be prepared for the unexpected. Knowing emergency numbers and where to seek help is essential, even if you don't plan on needing it.

Emergency Numbers:

- **Police**: 112

- **Fire Department**: 112

- **Ambulance**: 112

- **Tourist Police**: 116 000

- **Coast Guard**: 195 (useful if you're venturing out onto the water)

The Croatian emergency number is 112, which is a unified emergency services number, meaning it connects you to the police, fire department, or ambulance based on the situation. For tourists, the Tourist Police number is a particularly useful resource. If you lose your passport, wallet, or run into any issues during your travels, don't hesitate to reach out to them.

Tourist Help Lines:

- **Croatian National Tourist Board**: +385 1 469 9600

- **Zadar Tourist Information Center**: +385 23 202 040

These help lines are available for general tourist inquiries, guidance on local attractions, and urgent matters. They can assist with directions, recommendations, and more, ensuring you always have someone to turn to for reliable advice.

24.2 Recommended Books, Guides & Websites

If you're looking to deepen your understanding of Zadar or Croatia, these resources will not only enrich your trip but also help you plan your travels effectively.

Books & Guides:

- *"The Rough Guide to Croatia"* – A comprehensive guide that covers everything from the best beaches to cultural events.

- *"Rick Steves Croatia & Slovenia"* – A well-rounded guide with practical tips, itinerary suggestions, and insights into local culture and history.

- *"Lonely Planet Croatia"* – An extensive guide known for its depth of coverage and up-to-date information on accommodations, restaurants, and attractions.

Websites:

- **Croatian National Tourist Board (CNTB)**: www.croatia.hr

- **Zadar Tourist Information**: www.tzzadar.hr

- **Visit Croatia**: www.visit-croatia.co.uk

These resources will keep you updated on events, festivals, and practical travel tips. Make sure to consult them before and during your travels to stay in the loop.

24.3 Croatian Language Essentials (Key Phrases)

While many people in Zadar speak English, especially in tourist areas, learning a few basic Croatian phrases can go a long way in enriching your experience. It shows respect for the local culture and can help you connect more meaningfully with the people you meet.

Here are some essential Croatian phrases you might find useful:

- **Hello** – *Bok* (informal) / *Dobar dan* (formal, good day)

- **Goodbye** – *Doviđenja*

- **Please** – *Molim*

- **Thank you** – *Hvala*

- **Yes** – *Da*

- **No** – *Ne*

- **Excuse me / Sorry** – *Oprostite*

- **How much does this cost?** – *Koliko ovo košta?*

- **Where is the bathroom?** – *Gdje je WC?*

- **I don't speak Croatian** – *Ne govorim hrvatski*

- **Can you help me?** – *Možete li mi pomoći?*

A little effort in speaking the local language is always appreciated, and these simple words will make your experience that much more authentic.

24.4 Tourist Info Centers & Key Locations

Zadar offers several tourist information centers where you can gather maps, book tours, and get advice from friendly locals. Here are a few key locations:

1. **Zadar Tourist Information Center (City Center)**

   o Located in the heart of the old town, this is your first stop for city maps, brochures, and information about current events and festivals.

   o Address: Trg pet bunara 1, Zadar

2. **Zadar Airport Tourist Information**

   o If you're flying in or out, make sure to stop by the airport information desk. It's small but very helpful, offering info on airport transfers, local transportation, and more.

   o Address: Zadar International Airport, Zemunik Donji

3. **Marina Zadar Tourist Center**

   o For those arriving by boat, this center is a great spot to get detailed information about local sailing and coastal tours.

   o Address: Ulica Ivana Mažuranića, Zadar

24.5 Calendar of Public Holidays & Festivals

To make the most of your trip to Zadar, it's helpful to know when public holidays and festivals take place. These events offer a glimpse into local traditions and are often an exciting way to experience the culture.

Public Holidays:

- **New Year's Day** – January 1

- **Easter** – Date varies (usually in March or April)

- **Labor Day** – May 1

- **Independence Day** – August 5

- **Christmas** – December 25

- **St. Stephen's Day** – December 26

Festivals:

- **Zadar Summer Festival** (June–August): A celebration of music, theater, and dance that takes place in various venues around the city.

- **Zadar Music Festival** (July–August): A classical music event, bringing together world-renowned musicians for stunning performances.

- **The Zadar Advent** (December): The old town is transformed into a Christmas wonderland, with markets, lights, and festive concerts.

Plan your visit around these dates if you want to be part of the action, or if you prefer a quieter experience, consider traveling during the shoulder seasons.

24.6 Maps, Transit Schedules & City Layout

Having a good map and knowing how to get around Zadar will help you maximize your time exploring. The city is compact and easy to navigate on foot, but here are a few important details:

- **City Layout**: Zadar's Old Town is the heart of the city, with narrow cobbled streets and historical sites. The city is divided into districts, with the Old Town located on a small peninsula.

The Riva (seafront promenade) stretches along the western edge of the peninsula, offering stunning views of the sea and islands.

- **Transit**: Zadar's public transportation system is reliable and easy to use. Buses are the primary mode of transport, and tickets can be purchased on board or at kiosks. For trips to nearby destinations or airports, the shuttle services run regularly.

- **Maps**: Zadar Tourist Information Centers offer free maps, and the Google Maps app is incredibly useful for real-time navigation.

24.7 Helpful Apps for Travel in Croatia

Traveling in Croatia has become more convenient with the rise of helpful apps that guide you through the country. Here are a few must-have apps:

- **Google Maps**: Essential for navigating Zadar's winding streets and finding your way around public transportation.

- **Uber**: Available in Zadar for easy and affordable rides around the city.

- **Moovit**: This app provides up-to-date bus and public transport schedules in Zadar and other Croatian cities.

- **Croatia Travel Guide by Triposo**: Offers detailed guides on the best things to do in Croatia, including Zadar, with offline capabilities.

- **Split and Zadar Ferry Timetable**: If you plan on visiting nearby islands, this app is vital for checking ferry schedules.

Armed with these essential resources, you'll be well-equipped for a smooth and unforgettable experience in Zadar. Whether you need emergency contacts, local tips, or guidance on where to find the best local goods, this appendix ensures that you have everything you need to enjoy your travels fully. Safe travels, and may your journey in Croatia continue to be a story worth telling for years to come!

Printed in Dunstable, United Kingdom

63986941R00107